From Darkness to Light

Mai Tran's Journey of Passion

As told to Ray Martinez

Chico
PUBLISHING

Fort Collins, Colorado

First printing 2009
Printed and bound in the United States of America.

ISBN-13: 978-0-9644652-6-8 (paper back/trade paper)
ISBN-13: 978-0-9644652-7-5 (hardback/trade cloth)

Library of Congress Control Number: 2009905044

Chico PUBLISHING

Assisted in editing: Martha Williams Nichols, aMuse Productions®

www.raymartinez.com
DBA: RM Consulting, Inc.

Dedication

This book is dedicated to my mother, Khue Thi Vo, and my father, Be Van Tran. Their wisdom and courage of sacrificing everything they possessed, financially, and all of their love for us that provided each one of their children the opportunity to experience freedom and the chance to receive an education. Our success is a direct result of their sacrifice and intuitive insight of our future.

Thu-Hong and Mai Tran being held by their parents during a family dinner..

Table of Contents

Foreword

Mai A. Tran is the co-founder and majority owner of ITX (Information Technology eXperts). Since 1996, his company has achieved a remarkable 31% annual average growth rate. As president and CEO, Tran's areas of responsibility include overall customer service, technical quality, business development, contracts, human resources, and finance.

He is also a courageous emigrant who arrived in America with nothing and parlayed a determined education into a life's work of helping many people in many ways.

Tran has a bachelor's degree in computer sci-

ence from Colorado State University. He has twenty years' experience in the technical aspects of information technology, such as system administration, database management, data migration and conversion, security, and networks. Under Tran's leadership, ITX is passionate about giving unprecedented customer service. He has been heard more than once to say, "I measure our success not by growth rate or revenues, but by how well we satisfy our customers."

When it comes to pricing business costs for nonprofit businesses and sponsorships to events, Tran's benevolence toward nonprofit organizations speaks for itself. His experience in the "school of hard knocks" has had an immeasurable effect on his view of people and their adaptability to difficulties. His business approach is to constantly pursue research and development applicable to his daily practices.

Mai's experiences, from escaping from Vietnam on a small vessel to subsequently living on an inhumane ship for six months, are both hard to believe and inspiring. His hardships and his handling of the adversity lend insight into the dignity he owns and the dignity and respect he shows employees, customers, and those facing difficulties.

Mai Tran met his wife, Sue, in high school; Sue was a sophomore, and Mai was a senior. They had their first child, Melanie, in 1988. As of this writing, Melanie is attending college. Their second child, Melissa, born in 1992, currently attends the same high school Mai and Sue attended.

From left to right: Melanie, Sue, Mai, and Melissa Tran family

Preface

Growing up in a tightly woven family that had political ties with South Vietnam, I found myself in a quandary—I would have to leave my family and my country. It was clear that if my family and our cultural heritage were to survive, I must escape and try to find a new life for my whole family—a new beginning. I never dreamed of being one of the boat people.

Before the Communist Party took over Vietnam on April 30, 1975, my life was quite fulfilling. My family led a pleasant and successful life, supported by house servants and with no worries about where the next meal was coming from. Does wealth have its place? Certainly, and in the life of my family, wealth helped create an opportunity to seek freedom in another country. Yet, even today, I long to economically support my homeland. Perhaps my journey of passion, which began with uncertainty and hardship, helped set the stage to create a strong economic base and help an orphanage survive—actions that provided a real purpose and added meaning to life. To reach my dream, I had to escape and create a new life, not just for me, but also for many families here and abroad. My story is not merely a personal story, but it is a success story for many people. Most importantly, my passion drove me to the light of success.

The sudden takeover by the Communists had tremendous consequences for me as a young boy and the rest of my family. This dark period clouded our future. My father had been the Consulate for Vietnam in Thailand, but that was the past. In my family, there was an air of threat and imminent need to survive, and it wasn't safe to stay in South Vietnam anymore. On January 8, 1979, the time was right to escape. My sister and I were very young teenagers when the two of us left. The whole family attempted to escape three times unsuccessfully. On our fourth try to get out of the country, just Thu-Hong and I made it to the ship *Skyluck* after traveling in a small fishing vessel. The six months of anguish and dreadful living conditions on a small fishing vessel and the *Skyluck* left lasting memories of survival lessons—lessons and life skills that continue to serve a successful life journey.

With some streak of luck, coincidence, or "being there at the right time and place," my sister and I were sent to America and taken in by a big family from Fort Collins, Colorado. That family supported and raised us until we were on our own. Today, my company has 140 employees. My sister, Thu-Hong, who escaped together with me, is an electrical engineer in Fort Collins, and my other sister, Thu-Nga, who escaped one year later, is a doctor currently practicing internal medicine for Kaiser in Irvine, California. My family was certainly worth rescuing.

There are many stories like mine—but mine is one of those success stories we have the fortune to capture and put in writing. The following are some statistics that give you an idea of the enormity of trials and tribulations of the boat people:

Vietnam, Post-War Communist Regime (1975 et seq.): 430,000

- **Jacqueline Desbarats and Karl Jackson ("Vietnam 1975–1982: The Cruel Peace," in** *The Washington Quarterly*, **Fall 1985) estimated that there had been about 65,000 executions. This number is repeated in the September 1985** *Dept. of State Bulletin* **article on Vietnam.**

- *Orange County Register* **(29 April 2001): 1 million sent to camps and 165,000 died.**

- *Northwest Asian Weekly* **(5 July 1996): 150,000–175,000 camp prisoners unaccounted for.**

Estimates for the number of boat people who died:

- Elizabeth Becker (*When the War Was Over*, 1986) cites the UN High Commissioner on Refugees: 250,000 boat people died at sea; 929,600 reached asylum.

- The 20 July 1986 *San Diego Union-Tribune* cites the UN High Commissioner on Refugees: 200,000 to 250,000 boat people had died at sea since 1975.

- The 3 August 1979 *Washington Post* cites the Australian Immigration Minister's estimate that 200,000 refugees had died at sea since 1975. In addition, "Some estimates have said that around half of those who set out do not survive."

- The *1991 Information Please Almanac* cites unspecified "U.S. officials" as saying that 100,000 boat people died fleeing Vietnam.

- *Encarta* estimates that half a million fled and 10%–15% died, for a death toll of 50,000–75,000.

- Nayan Chanda, *Brother Enemy* (1986): A quarter million Chinese refugees in two years, 30,000 to 40,000 of whom died at sea. (Marilyn Young also repeats these numbers: *The Vietnam Wars: 1945-1990* (1991).)

http://boatpeople75.tripod.com/

1

I Remember My Homeland

I was one of six siblings—four sisters and one brother; I am the oldest son. Little did I know that I would not live forever in my homeland of Vietnam, but that I was destined for another country. My life there was fulfilling in the sense of family, wealth, and happiness. My sister, Thu-Hong, is a living witness to my trials during our lives. The two of us would make the great escape from Vietnam to America together, where we would realize the dark valley we would have to walk through to see the light.

I grew up in Saigon in the area known as District Three. Saigon is divided up into five districts: District One is the business area; District Two is the Villa section of town; District Three is the residential homes; District Four is mostly manufacturing; and District Five is known as China Town.

My parents were always special to me. My father, Be Van Tran, worked at the Vietnam Embassy in Thailand in a town called Nong

While I was writing this book, Mai and I met dozens of times to talk about his childhood and his life today. One of the things I noticed, as he reflected and reminisced, was that his facial expressions were like a light switch; when he was happy and enjoying telling his story, he spoke passionately and constantly smiled while looking directly at me. However, when he spoke about times of disappointment, Mai always looked down and away, as if he were tossing away those bad feelings and not wanting them to resurface. Conversely, when he talked about these life events as a source of learning and how they shaped him, Mai leaned forward and looked me straight in the eye. He spoke with diligence and determination, expressing tremendous feelings, as he recounted his life experiences. I also couldn't help but notice that Mai has an uncanny way of making a person laugh with him—his jubilant laugh will cause you to chuckle.

Khai, located in the northern part of the country near Laos. He was in charge of the consulate office for South Vietnam. He worked for the Vietnamese government for four years before the fall of South Vietnam. My mother, Khue Thi Vo—in the Vietnamese culture, the woman does not take the male spouse's last name—was a housewife, and when time allowed, she was also a produce commodities broker.

While I was growing up, I learned martial arts, particularly judo, which later came in handy for teaching a few American bullies a lesson about respect. On the other hand, judo lessons were an important way to learn about team building and developing relationships. Reflecting on times when I used to hang around with other neighborhood kids and how they managed to get into mischief, I realized even then those activities were *not* the best team-building experience.

I was not reared as a poor or hungry child, although poverty and hunger did exist there. Instead, I remember house servants and all the luxuries of life one could afford in Vietnam. I really didn't have to do anything—household chores, and so on. My family was middle-class in Vietnamese society. We had house servants, but they were not full-time employees for whom my parents had to pay taxes or offer a 401K plan. Instead, they were people making money on the side for extra cash who often ate lunch and dinner with us. Occasionally, a servant lived in our family home and received a monthly salary of some sort, along with room and board. The servant's job was to help with the kids, fix meals, and clean the house, usually accompanying us whenever our family traveled for business or leisure.

Quang (my only brother) is a computer network analyst. My sister, Thu-Van, graduated with a double major in math and French, and she is currently a stay-at-home mom raising two beautiful children. My sister, Thu, is a retired restaurant owner in Colorado. My entire immediate family now lives in the United States.

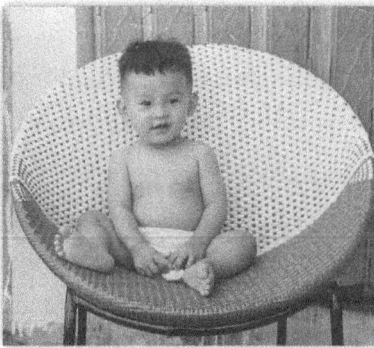

Mai was one year old when this photo was taken outside his home.

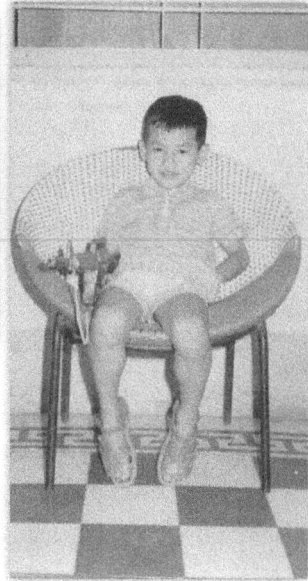

Mai sits in the same chair at age six.

I recall many times when Mom sent us kids outside into the streets early in the morning to get food from the various portable food vendors peddling food products—rice, noodles, etc. By ten o'clock in the morning, the vendors were gone. We were the first in our neighborhood to have television—this was in 1969. Being the first to have TV, we attracted thirty to forty neighbors into our home to be entertained by the two available channels. We were the hit of the neighborhood!

While we were in school, Mom usually went to the market to shop for more food. The schools in Vietnam are much more intense than in the U.S. School always started at eight o'clock, twelve o'clock, or six o'clock. Vietnam really utilized their school buildings. Some teachers worked two shifts. Each student attended one of the four-hour blocks of school, either in the morning, afternoon, or at night; Monday through Saturday. Compared to the all-day U.S. schools, we accomplished just as much in the Vietnamese half-day sessions. Vietnamese school supplies were limited to a ruler. Nothing such as compasses, protractors, calculators, or slide rules existed for us.

Our home was in a gated community, primarily because my father was with the foreign department and stationed in Thailand for four years. Dad's job changed in 1972, and he became a government auditor who investigated government improprieties in southern Vietnam.

My mother stayed home most of the time but occasionally worked in the Vietnamese stock market, particularly in rice commodities. We respected both parents equally, but Mom was usually the first person we went to for permission to do any special activity. My love for Mom had no bounds, and I had much respect for her drive to succeed in raising all of us while still working. She was a gem, more valuable than gold, and she was willing to part with my parents' actual gold to bring opportunities in life to us kids. More importantly, I know this was a hard and courageous decision for my mother to allow her children to leave solo to seek freedom by escaping from Vietnam, our homeland.

Mai Tran's home as it stands today—loft on the right side.

Dad was not always as involved with the kids' sports activities as we are in the United States. Very rarely did parents show up for ping-pong or soccer matches. Often, I played sports on the "quiet side"—without my parents knowing. They figured sports would diminish studying in school. Dad and Mom were mostly interested and invested in their children's education.

Fights among neighborhood kids were common and were often sparked by turf issues, similar to neighborhood fights in the United States. Fights ignited for many reasons—walking through the "wrong" neighborhood (where we or our companions did not live or belong) or because someone "looked funny." No one even had to say anything to each other—the fight just erupted. Several times, I was a victim of those attacks. I knew when I was in the wrong neighborhood, but my friends lived there, and I was willing to take the chance.

When there were high school rifts, you literally saw hundreds of kids

Mai Tran standing on the beach of 'Vung Tau' at age four.

running at each other from the two schools. The fights were very brief—and often over a sports rivalry—because the police quickly arrived. The rivalry fights were usually between one school that mostly had police officials' kids and my school, which was full of governmental officials' kids. There was no special connection between the conflicts and the families' professions; it just worked out that way.

Most of the time, the parents at home didn't know about the fights, but if they caught wind of it, you got a spanking. Dad most often handed down the discipline in our house. These spankings usually were done with a bamboo stick. You lay down on the ground, and Mom or Dad whipped your butt.

I considered myself a wild kid, and I was often disciplined for good reasons—mostly because I engaged in fights with other groups of boys. Several times, the police took me to the police station where my parents picked me up. Punishment awaited me at home. On other occasions, I was disciplined for missing school. When they said school started at 8:00 a.m., that was precisely what they meant. After that, the school doors were locked, and the teachers or administrators would not let children in if they were tardy. Because I was not fond of school, I deliberately locked myself in the bathroom at home until eight o'clock to avoid attending class.

The rest of my siblings were very good students and always ranked in the top five students of their class. As for me, I always ranked in the middle of the class. I did work *not* to be at the bottom, because I knew that would mean trouble at home, but I definitely wasn't striving to be at the top of the class. I just didn't care about school.

I searched for reasons I didn't want to attend school, such as not liking my teacher. My parents would take me outside our home and show me people doing manual labor—hard labor, which most people didn't like. They pointed out to me that I would be doing the same if I did not stay in school. However, it didn't register with me at that age and with my life history and situation to that point; I realized the value later in life, so I only did enough homework to get by.

Students always wore uniforms for school: white shirt, blue shorts, and slippers. When playing sports, the kids often played soccer barefooted. It was just too hot to wear shoes.

I valued family, and one of the strongest traditions within my family was (and is) respect. It was important to respect your parents and older folks, as well as those people in need. Dad and Mom traditionally helped poor people with donations of food or money. Even at times when they didn't have much money, my parents would borrow money to help others.

As I have said, the kids in my family really did not have to work, and we were not expected to do chores. The servants literally catered to all our needs. If we wanted a second bowl of food, the servant prepared it for us without our having to get up from the dinner table.

The first time I ever had a job was when the Communists took over Vietnam, and I fled from Vietnam to Hong Kong. The journey from Vietnam to Hong Kong on the *Skyluck* was harsh, and I learned critical work skills while in survival mode on that ship, which had become a floating city with a market for bartering and trading for food or gold some might be traveling with; everyone seemed to have something to trade or sell. Therefore, when I arrived in Hong Kong, the necessity to work did not shock me. Intuitively and instinctively, I knew this was the only way to survive—by working and quickly learning whatever there was to learn. I became like a sponge, receptive to all my surroundings.

My first job in Hong Kong was carrying heavy wooden crates of bottled products. I knew deep down inside that this kind of heavy labor was not for me; the experience created a stronger incentive for me to secure a quality education. I viewed these physical jobs in Hong Kong and the United States as merely a step toward my goal of education.

I loved my parents, but in our culture, feelings are not always openly expressed. Care is expressed by telling them that you love them but more so, by what you *do* for them. The great escape, and what it enabled me to do for my family, is certainly a clear expression of my love for my entire family. The government might change, but family remains the same.

2

Communism Changed Our Lifestyle

When the new Communist government took over, the old regime had to flee the country. The organizers of the great escape were people from the small town called *Bến Tre*. This little community bribed the Communists to close their eyes to the people who wanted to escape. The people who had to escape were the Vietnamese, not the half-Chinese and half-Vietnamese people. The Vietnamese people of the south were in conflict with the Communist government. The indigenous Vietnamese were told to leave.

Soon after the Vietnam War ended in 1975, the Vietcong military reunited the northern and southern parts of the country. Naturally, people fled out of fear of the new Communist government. Some escaped across the border into Thailand, while others fled by boat into Malaysia, Indonesia, Singapore, and Hong Kong. The Vietcong started the "ethnic cleansing" in major cities in Vietnam, causing Chinese Vietnamese to flee to Hong Kong.

For our family to escape, we would have to pay an enticement fee. The bribe was not cheap for the Vietnamese—8 one-ounce bars of gold per child. Suddenly, my father and mother no longer had the influence they used to wield. Our family was in survival mode, and we were not free to travel to certain areas in our own country. We feared retribution for my parents' support and employment by the previous regime.

With mixed feelings, I remember a moment when Mom showed us all the gold she and Dad had saved for emergencies such as this—the need to escape for political reasons. The gold was carefully hidden and protected. When my mother told us to look at the gold, she said, "Look at this gold now, because you will never see it again," implying that the gold would be used to help us escape and save all our futures.

The war between Vietnam and China in 1978 was over a land dispute, and it became a driving force for our family to go into exile. China backed Ha-

Mai Tran was twelve years old when this photo was taken in Saigon.

noi during the Vietnam War; consequently, they wanted to punish Vietnam for invading Cambodia in 1978 and ousting the genocidal Khmer Rouge regime of Pol Pot, the radical Maoist leader Beijing backed. On December 1, 2009, the *Sidney Morning Herald* reported that the longstanding land dispute had been settled on New Year's Eve (December 31, 2008). February 2009 would mark thirty years since China invaded Vietnam.

During this time, the Vietnam government demanded that all Chinese, half-Chinese, or half-Vietnamese leave the country. After several failed attempts for us all to escape together, our family lost all our gold. My parents ran out of money sources. Fortunately, my aunt loaned my mom just enough gold to pay the fee for two kids to escape. My sister, Thu-Hong, and I were the chosen ones among six siblings to escape and seek a better future and acquire an education.

While I listened to Mai describe his early experiences, I couldn't help but think about my own circumstance at age fifteen—I was just entering high school, smoking cigarettes, and living through a rebellious stage of my own. By the time Mai was on his journey to America, I was a young police officer, patrolling the streets of Fort Collins. I often thought of these two radically different circumstances while writing and piecing this story together.

Thu-Hong and I took advantage of the opportunity to escape with the Chinese, even though we were full-blooded Vietnamese. This was a daunting challenge for us because we were so young, barely in our teens, when we made the great escape.

To this day, I view family values in Vietnam as much stronger and close-knit than in the United States. In American society, we tend to place our parents in nursing homes after a certain point in life. You don't see very many nursing homes in Vietnam. It's the family's responsibility to care for its own aging family. Vietnam doesn't have a Social Security program as in the United States. The welfare program in Vietnam is the kids caring for their own family; whereas here in the U.S., we ask the government to take care of our aging parents (clearly, not in all cases).

John E. Carey wrote an interesting story on Peace and Freedom II. It is on the Internet at *http://johnibii.wordpress.com/2007/08/20/ new-arrival-from-vietnam-talks-about-communism/*. He writes about his interview with Thieu, who grew up in Vietnam and who was a professional teacher of literature and history. After the Communists took over all of Vietnam in 1975, Thieu fell in love with and married a woman working for the Communist government. Thieu was asked to think a moment and tell Carey the worst aspect of Communism. Thieu did think, but only for a moment, and then said, "Communist governments always lie."

> Vietnam was divided, with Ho in power in the North and Ngo Dinh Diem, a Roman Catholic anti-Communist in a largely Buddhist population, heading the government in the South. Elections were to be held two years later to unify the country. Persuaded that the fall of Vietnam could lead to the fall of Burma, Thailand, and Indonesia, Eisenhower backed Diem's refusal to hold elections in 1956 and effectively established South Vietnam as an American client state.

> Kennedy increased assistance, and sent a small number of military advisors, but a new guerrilla struggle between North and South continued. Diem's unpopularity grew and the military situation wors-

ened. In late 1963, Kennedy secretly assented to a coup d'état. To the president's surprise, Diem and his powerful brother-in-law, Ngo Dien Nu, were killed. It was at this uncertain juncture that Kennedy's presidency ended three weeks later. (http://usinfo.state.gov/products/pubs/histryotln/decades.htm)

Another article to read is in the *National Review* (April 29, 1977, page 487, or *http://jim.com/ChomskyLiesCites/When_we_knew_what_happened_in_Vietnam.htm*) called "The New Vietnam."

Was the change scary? Did a person wonder what might happen from day to day? When Communism was enacted, there was immediate fear among the people. It seemed as if no one talked to each other—the community became quiet because people worried about who could be watching. I remember seeing the police remove people from their homes in the middle of the night, and of course, I heard rumors about many others being taken away. Without knowing why, people were concerned that perhaps their family would be next for the police to remove and sequester. Most businesses in the area shut down, probably out of fear of a government coup—a bleak image of worrisome people vacating Vietnam's streets during the first week of the Communist takeover.

Suddenly, neighbors were carrying guns—arming themselves to feel safe—but were they safe? I could sense the fear in my parents—fear of the unknown—yet realizing my father was a government employee under the old regime, which might or might not afford the family some security. For a whole month, kids didn't attend school. People shut themselves inside their homes, limiting where they walked or traveled. They must have pondered daily about what might be in store for them.

There was now a definite lack of trust in the community where I lived. We didn't trust personal conversations with our friends, neighbors, teachers, and others—not knowing who would or could report us to the authorities.

The government was the last entity to trust. There were no laws to follow. Parents were cautious about telling their children about their feelings for fear that the kids might inadvertently say something wrong to their friends or teachers. Of course, my parents did not worry about the loyalty of our family, but sometimes a slip of the tongue at the wrong time can convey a misleading message to another's ears. We, in America, know how easily the media can misinterpret what people say. All Vietnamese knew an old Vietnamese proverb "Phep vua thua le lang" (the laws of the emperor yield to the customs of the village). In many respects, it characterized the village in Vietnam as a self-contained homogenous community, jealously guarding its way of life, creating an autonomous little world that disregarded (if not disdained) the outside world (Gerald Cannon Hickey, Village in Vietnam, New Haven: Yale University Press, 1964, p. 276). However, now that the people were falling into the hands of the Communists, would the emperor really yield to their village's customs?

Everyone's freedom was in jeopardy. You were not allowed to travel without permission or even stay at a friend's home without filling out a travel request with the local police. You certainly didn't have freedom of speech, especially regarding politics.

Even music was censored. No one was allowed to listen to love story lyrics or religious music. The new government provided the only music allowed. I recall listening to music with a friend while hiding in the attic of my friend's home—and yes, it was hotter than hell. Back then, we used an old turntable phonograph. Nevertheless, we cautiously listened to my friend's music in spite of the new regime's rigid standards. Why was it so important to control the music anyone listened to for entertainment? How in the world do you enjoy music under the potential threat of incarceration?

Luxury was not a luxury. For example, eating chicken was considered upper-class. The communist restricted all forms of luxury. So, when we did eat chicken, after butchering a chicken in the house, we made sure not one discoverable feather was left behind. My parents were not allowed to keep their personal car—they were forced to donate it to the police. There was a lot of giving-up, as we saw our culture change through the governing Communists' unyielding control.

Our family knew we had to escape and rebuild our lives in a free country.

3

The Three Attempted Escapes

It was urgent for our family to escape to freedom somehow, some way. According to the free media, Wikipedia.org, events resulting from the Vietnam War caused many people in Cambodia, Laos, and especially, Vietnam, to become refugees in the late 1970s and 1980s, particularly after the fall of Saigon. In Vietnam, the new Communist government sent many people supporting the old government in the South to "re-education camps" and others to "new economic zones." An estimated 1 million people were imprisoned without formal charges or trials.

According to published academic studies in the United States and Europe, 165,000 people died in the Socialist Republic of Vietnam's re-education camps. Thousands were abused or tortured. These factors, coupled with poverty, caused hundreds of thousands of Vietnamese to flee the country.

In 1979, Vietnam was at war (<u>Sino-Vietnamese War</u>) with the <u>People's Republic of China</u> (PRC). Many <u>ethnic Chinese</u> in Vietnam felt that the government's policies directly targeted them, and they became "boat people."On the open seas, not only did boat people have to contend with harsh conditions on board, but they also confronted the forces of nature and had to elude <u>pirates</u>.

In Cambodia, the <u>Khmer Rouge</u> regime murdered millions of people in the "<u>Killing Fields</u>" massacres. Many people attempted to escape, but few were successful.

Trying to escape Vietnam was a risky and trying undertaking, full of false hopes, disappointments, and fraud. Escape attempts were often expensive and often resulted in con artists defrauding hapless people of their money. On some occasions, people were told that they could escape, but money was always required up front with limited assurance that their escape would succeed. All funding was paid in gold, no paper money. People usually had to give half down, which was about five to six thousand dollars in gold.

Mai poses for a family picture at Vang Tau Beach (a popular tourist area in Vietnam) just before his escape.

In 1976, 1977, and 1978, my family's attempts to escape were to no avail—and with no refund of our money. After these three attempts, my parents decided it was too hard to attempt as an entire family—too risky and too expensive. It was more important to them that at least part of the family escape, and they hoped it would work out for them all later. However, when I was told the plan, I had no assurance my parents would successfully make the great escape. With mixed emotions, I realized that, once I escaped, I might never see my family again and, of course, probably never go back to my homeland, Vietnam.

In previous attempts to leave as a family, the assumed brokers came to our home to tell us in what town we were to meet them. We were always prepared to leave in a hurry. Small amounts of clothing and essentials were always packed and ready to leave on a bus, train, or motorcycle in the middle of the night.

During the first escape attempt in 1976, my cousin was working with my mother,—yes, Mom planned and designed these attempted escapes. My cousin had the connections for the boat ride, and she collected the money to pay for the attempt. The plan was to escape within three to six months. Naturally, my parents paid in advance, a whopping ten ounces of gold per person, meaning it was about $3,000 per person. It took about three months to get a response or notification that their attempt to escape was imminent. We got three-days notice that the first attempt would soon occur. Our cousin notified my mother that someone would pick us up at 10:30 p.m. to take us to the train station. Knowing that we were going soon, we all soaked up the sun, so we could blend in with the fishing community by the coast. The night of the escape, we rode the train all night and arrived in Phan Thiet at 5:00 a.m. For survival

Mai's mother (Khue Thi Vo) and father (Be Van Tran)
now live in the United States.

reasons, we never stayed together. Even on the train, we split up and traveled in different cars. I remember my brother, Quang, who was only three years old then; Quang stayed with Mom during the split-up on the train and in Phan Thiet. (Today, Quang works with me at my company ITX [Information Technology eXperts].)

When we exited the train, we saw each other, but we wouldn't talk to one another for fear people would mark us as a family, signaling the police we might be trying to escape. We waited near the train station for another pick-up to take us to a relay house. After waiting until noon the same day, we realized that perhaps no one was going to pick us up for the next transport to the boat. Finally, Mom made the decision to return home, telling the family that the police caught the couriers.

And so, the first attempted escape was aborted. There was a rush to get back home, knowing that the police would seize our home once it was abandoned for more than twenty-four hours. When we arrived home after a lengthy train ride, Mom realized that my two sisters, Thu and Thu-Van, ages 19 and 16 years, were missing. In any case, we continued our journey home, as time was of the essence. Instinctively, we knew better than to arrive home all at once. We knew the importance of trickling our way back, so the police wouldn't know we were traveling as a family.

Upon arriving home, we discovered that the police were already inventorying our home. Dad told the police we had not abandoned our home. He explained that we left because of a family illness, claiming that our grandmother was sick. The police accepted our excuse, although the neighbors obviously had told the police that we left. That was why you didn't trust anyone. People learned not to tell others of family plans or even about personal life stories.

The next day, Mom traveled alone back to Phan Thiet to look for the girls who were still missing. She went directly to the police station in Phan Thiet, where she discovered that my sisters were in jail. Mom had to pay bribery money to get them out of jail, telling the police that the girls "ran away from home" with other friends. Subsequently, the girls were home within a couple of days.

One has to wonder how and why the police picked up the girls. I suspect that the police saw the two of them wandering around aimlessly. The police probably knew most people in the town and saw these girls as strangers. Naturally, the police inquired about where they lived and who their family was, and with each question, a lack of consistency led to the lack of veracity and the subsequent arrest by the police.

During the second "escape" in 1977—about four to six months later—we left for the same town, Phan Thiet, and the same route of travel. We were able to use the same gold as last time. The gold had been returned because of the failed escape attempt, which rarely happened. The same principles were used to prepare for the escape. This attempt almost mirrored the first attempt. No one picked us up at the train station to take my family to another hideaway. Everyone just returned home with some speculation that perhaps this was a fraud. However, a mixture of desperation and hope kept alive the belief it had been a legitimate attempt.

In 1978—the third attempt—we again used the same gold for payment. This time, no one picked us up at home. Our cousin, the organizer, was responsible for organizing several families for this escape. It was hard to believe, but our cousin abandoned us and took the gold our family had paid up front. A couple of days later, about half the gold was returned to my parents through a cousin's friend. Mom was very upset and panicked that she and Dad had been "cheated," and they might not get the rest of their gold back.

This third escape was devastating. Not only was our family abandoned, but also our family's friends were left behind. In our culture, we knew that if our cousin were found, other families would take revenge. However, one week later, we found out that the police in Phan Thiet had caught our cousin and the people who escaped, while traveling to the "beach front" to climb aboard a boat.

Phan Thiet is located in Binh Thuan Province. It is 200 km from Saigon and lies south of Cam Ranh Bay on the southernmost stretch of central Vietnam. Binh Thuan was once part of the Cham Kingdom. In 1692, Lord Nguyen Phuc Chu captured the area and named it Binh Thuan Dinh. Binh Thuan is quite important in Vietnam's history, as it was in this area in 1306 that King Tran Nhan Tong agreed to the marriage of Princess Huyen Chan to King Jaya Sinhavarman III of the Cham Kingdom. During the revolution against the French, it was in this area that the two patriots Phan Chu Trinh and Tran Quy Cap had their start. Furthermore, according to local lore, the area around Phan Thiet is where Han Mac Tu, the disfigured poet, spent his time forlornly, as he waited for Mong Cam, the woman of his dreams. Today, Phan Thiet is the largest town in Binh Thuan province with an estimated population of about 100,000 people. (*http://www.vietscape.com/travel/phanthiet/index.html*)

Remember, this attempt involved going to a hideaway house after the train ride. Once we were at the hideaway house, they waited until nightfall, when they took about one hundred people to the "beach front." People would climb into several handmade floating bamboo baskets. The plan was to paddle to a fishing boat. However, they had to signal the boat with a flashlight, so the boat hands would know the baskets were on their way and retrieve them from the water. This particular attempt by my cousin was foiled because of a lack of communication—the boat didn't see their signal because of the high waves. Consequently, the baskets were not sent to them. My cousin and others spent the night on the beach.

Suddenly, they saw a village boy coming to the beach to catch clams. Fearing he would report them to the police, they kidnapped him, holding him while waiting for their escape. But the boy raised such a fuss and cried, so they let him go, hoping he wouldn't say anything. Much to their dismay, the village boy reported the band of people to the police.

When they noticed the police approaching, the people scrambled to bury their gold in the sand, so the police wouldn't seize it.

The police knew that the more gold you had in your possession, the more trouble you were in with the Vietnamese government. So, it was a blessing we didn't go on this third trip; otherwise, we would have been caught.

The fourth escape required a new plan of action. Although three attempts had already failed, the next attempt would be successful. This time, only two of us were left.

From left, Mai and his siblings: Quang, Thu-nga, Thu-Hong, Thu-Van, Thu, and Mai Tran. Quang and Thu were later sponsored to the United States. Thu-nga and Thu-Van escaped one year after Mai and Thu-Hong initially escaped together.

4

The Successful Escape from Vietnam

In 1979, my parents chose my sister and me out of the rest of the siblings to escape because we were the middle children. The youngest, Quang, was only four or five years old. During the war between the Vietnamese and the Chinese in North Vietnam, the military draft age was seventeen, and I was approaching it. This war was over border disputes. Some of our family friends were involved in the conflict, and their sons never made it back home. Consequently, Dad and Mom did not want to risk sending their oldest son to war. My parents picked the younger of the sisters, Thu-Hong, because she really wanted to go with me. Even though I was closer with my older sister, the decision to send Thu-Hong was final. This great escape drew the two of us closer together—bonding in the works. Of course, the ultimate goal was for the entire family to escape.

I never had second thoughts of retreating because remaining in our homeland meant more risks and disregarding what my parents

No one knew how many attempted escapes Mai was going to endure. Little did he know this was going to be the escape that worked! Yet, in his mind, he knew that nothing was a sure deal until it was over. Mai always exhibited a strong persona and a will to achieve whatever he believed. His determination is not only an integral part of his inner convictions, but his expression paints a picture of a bulldozer barreling, regardless of the circumstance, through walls or barriers that he has to break.

Geographically, Bến Tre, Vietnam, is wedged between the two main branches of the Tiền Giang River, which is one of the two main branches of the Mekong. It was a secluded site where many Vietnamese waited for the opportunity to leave. While waiting in Bến Tre, word reached us that

wanted. I knew it was the only way to build a future somewhere in a free land. We didn't know which, what, or where this land of freedom was, nor did we know our final destination. Unknown to us, this was going to be a harsh and perplexing experience.

Finally, the word came through a messenger, and we dashed for the boat. When we saw the boat all were scrambling to board, it was shocking, and it made us wonder if this were at all possible. But I was determined that we would somehow squeeze on.

The boat was a small fishing boat capable of holding fifteen people. The person in charge of loading the boat managed, through sheer desperation and grit, to force three hundred people on this fishing vessel!

Can you imagine the clamoring, pushing, and shoving going on while trying to fit, sit, or stand? It was chaotic—so much for a quiet voyage. The movement of the seawaters was unsettling. Every swell caused a shift with our seating arrangements. Nevertheless, every slap of the waves against our boat meant we were further separated from home and moving toward a chance of freedom. We were that much closer to sovereignty. Someone once said, "A ship is safe at shore, but that's not where a ship belongs."

Confined on a fisherman's vessel, we quickly learned to adapt from our former wealthy lifestyle with the luxury of a home, servants, and friends to cramped quarters, seeing to ourselves, and being surrounded by strangers. For the two of us, at such young ages, this was a new vista and venture. Most kids at this age were doing something such as that for a great experience—something to put on a résumé. We, however, were venturing out for survival, never forgetting where we came from and hoping to reunite someday with our family. Yet, we understood that we might never see our beloved family again.

Mai and Thu-Hong would be picked up in ten to fifteen minutes. Bến Tre contained a smaller village known as Binh dai, in which about 1,000 people lived. Mai and his sister were now separated from the rest of their family, and they knew this departure was the final separation for an unknown period—perhaps forever. Mai assumed that he would not see his family again. There was an even chance that their journey would have a catastrophic ending or be a success. There were no other options. It was like that old saying, "sink or swim."

Looking at this fishing vessel must have been like looking at the ship inside the bottle. How did the model ship get inside the bottle that had such a small neck? The answer: piece by piece, and yes, for these children, it was step by step.

Leaving home with only two sets of clothing stuffed in a cloth bag made by our mother gave Thu-Hong and me a feeling of starting life all over again. The written name and address of friends in the United States inside our cloth carrying bag signaled there was only one way to go, and it wasn't back to Vietnam.

My hope was an enduring resolution to an interim dilemma. This

small fishing vessel would soon be traded for a large ship, but the
boat lifestyle didn't necessarily improve for us on the *Skyluck*.

*Mai pictured here with his school friends, leaving them
behind to escape for freedom. Mai is the second person
from the right (age sixteen)."*

5

The *Skyluck*

When Thu-Hong and I desperately climbed into the small fishing vessel, we had no idea how long we would be at sea in such cramped conditions. I estimate that we traveled about seven to eight hours. People were seasick, vomiting on each other, and Thu-Hong and I got the brunt of the "outfall" because we were sitting on the vessel's bottom level. There was very little air to breathe and barely enough room to sit. In no way could we straighten our legs. What do you talk about for eight hours with strangers bumped up next to you?

Finally, the vessel reached the big *Skyluck*. We didn't know it, but the *Skyluck* was a commercial ship from Panama. The ship was designed to carry large paper rolls, not passengers. While approaching the big ship, we saw several fishing boats full of people heading for the same ship. Questions were racing through my mind: Will we get on? Will they turn us away—all this for nothing? What else could possibly go wrong?

Between 1978 and 1981, a daily average of 150 Vietnamese refugees arrived at Hong Kong in small or large boats. The Skyluck was the big vessel that carried Mai and his sister into Hong Kong harbor after twenty-one days at sea. They assumed this was their final destination to freedom.

This freighter, the 3,500-ton Skyluck, will go down in Hong Kong history as the refugee ship that took a "short cut" to freedom. The Panamanian-registered Skyluck disregarded the authorities by quietly slipping into Hong Kong unannounced. The ship stole into port during the early hours of Wednesday, February 8, 1979, with a human cargo of 2,700 desperate Vietnamese refugees. Other pictures of the Skyluck can be seen at http://www.library.ubc.ca/asian/FinalAsian/Vietnam/V-17.html and

http://www.library.ubc.ca/asian/FinalAsian/Vietnam/V-10.html .

Hours went by until the vessel approached the boarding dock. Standing up wasn't easy—cramped legs and dizziness were the first sensations, as we prepared to stand and leave the fishing vessel. Finally, our feet touched the platform of the *Skyluck*. I felt successful! After all, I was on the big ship that would take us to our final destination and *freedom*, right?

Skyluck had many nooks and crannies. It was designed to carry about 650 people, mostly laborers to manage the cargo. Somehow, about 2,700 people squeezed onboard the ship—all Vietnamese refugees. Who was in charge? There was a race to find places to sit and lie down for the long journey ahead. Everyone on the ship knew they were in for a long haul and again were to face few conveniences and very little comfort.

We had no idea where the ship was going. We rode and sat on large spools of stacked newsprint rolls. This was our home for the next six months—where we ate, slept, and socialized. Lavatory facilities didn't exist. Human waste disposal was "handled" by using the ship's onboard crane that suspended a netted rope basket with a board on the bottom for people to walk out and stand on. The crane swung the netted basket over the ocean, where people released their bodily wastes. Those memories never go away.

For six months, we lived on a stack of large spools of paper. These were stacked so high that we could not stand up straight without hitting our heads on the ceiling of the sectional bin for paper storage.

Although we were confined to the ship, there was a market to sell food, exchange products, and so forth. Many people carried gold with them in case they needed it for their travels. Suddenly, the ship became a marketplace for trade, socializing, and planning our next maneuver to continue this great escape. Yes, a floating village searching for freedom—what was its next destiny?

Photograph taken and provided by Mr. Chan Kiu in Hong Kong, who is now living in Vancouver, Canada.

Mai's journey brought him to Colorado. In 1980, Mai kept a diary of his high school "Outward Bound trip." I noticed that, on his first night of camping outside, he reflected on his experience and wrote, "I sleep outside, we don't have a top for tonight, but I don't care because I am very tired and very cold. It is raining too. I can't sleep I miss my mom my sitter I want to go home it is not fun, it look like wen I lived on a boat." The next morning, when waking up to a new day, Mai expressed his confusion: "In a morning I get up 8 o'clock, I think I am in my room, I am wrong, I am in my sleep in bag. I miss my famille my mom, dad, very much…I can't see them now. We are eating breakfast with chocolat milk and some thing I can't eat because it is very new for me."

Throughout this book are my memories captured from my personal diary. They never go away. The diary documents the lasting impressions of my life lessons and emotions often echoing in my memory. Even the simplest experiences of listening to and feeling the rain fall on my sleeping bag invoke past pain. Nevertheless, I feel that the pain was well worth the outcome.

Perhaps this next stop would be our destination of freedom or at least another step in that direction.

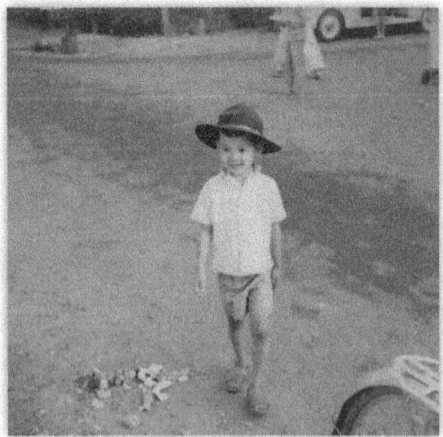

Pictured here, Mai Tran was age seven, walking around in his neighborhood. Little did he know, in eight years, he would be running for his life—figuring out how to survive.

6

The First Stop—The Philippines

Traveling in a crowded ship was grueling. It took seven or ten days to reach the Philippines, and we arrived during the night. Not willing to take any chances, the ship crept in by night to a nearby deserted island located near the Philippines. Everyone was wary about whether we would be welcomed.

Wasting no time, the refugees assembled themselves to exit quickly onto a smaller boat to take them to the deserted island. Each time the smaller boat returned, about five hundred people would exit the ship and board the small boat. No one had seen where we were traveling during the night. The night was eerie, with very little chatter, and all human senses were at their sharpest.

I suggested to my sister that we shouldn't line up to exit the ship yet. My instinct suggested that something could go wrong during the night. I thought it would be safer to exit during the daylight, so we could see where we were going.

I remembered looking through the handwritten diary Mai kept while attending a twenty-two-day Outward Bound trip in the Colorado mountains during high school in 1980. He reflected on his miserable ride on the Skyluck, comparing it to his first night of outdoor camping. Here is what Mai wrote, unedited with grammar and spelling as he wrote it. Keep in mind that he only had six months of "self-taught" English:

"...we start to go on a top of a mountain. I am very tired, I can't think I walk and carry 40 pounds. I walk about 6 hours and stop it at 8 o'clock. We eat sup but it is not look like a sup, after we ate we go to sleep in a sleep in bag." *This was his first diary entry of his twenty-two-day trip. Mai was writing to his foster mother in the United States.*

In another section of the same diary, Mai gives us a glimpse of his experience and emotions while on the Skyluck. He writes, "Dear Mom, tonight I want to write for you, I know you can't read what I am writing, but I _____ to write for

When daylight broke, it was our turn to exit onto the smaller boat. Suddenly, the Philippines Coast Guard started to chase the boat and the *Skyluck* away. Lucky for us, we were just getting ready to step onto the boat, standing by the ladder to get on. Without notice, the *Skyluck* started moving quickly. I quickly realized that this was an illegal dropping point; I couldn't know if the Coast Guard was going to seize our ship or not. When you are a fifteen-year-old boy, you have only limited life knowledge and experience to draw on, and you must rely on what your gut tells you to do to survive. I also knew that I must be strong for my sister.

We were off and running without rest or arrest. Who knew where we were going next? Living conditions were harsh and unhealthy. Food was only available once every twenty-four hours, and it was never consistent as to what time the "meal" occurred. The daily sustenance consisted of one bowl of rice soup *(here, Mai demonstrated for me by his cupped hands the small portion given to each person for*

you. I and my sittor, we left our famille almost 2 years, we are very sad. Six months we lived on a Skyluck. We met to many people not good. They hurt me and Thu (his sister) to much, when we were sicking, we didn't have any people help us. Th, she cryed very much, I wanted to cry too but, if I was crying I could not stop her crying. I was biger than I lived with my famille, I am stronger than I lived with my parents because I have Th my younger sittor. She is very soft and she doesn't know not thing I have to help and guardian her. 2 years ago we look like baby birds can't fly in big sky. Six months we lived on a ship..."

On his twelfth day of the camping trip, Mai writes about having to go solo for three days: "Last night we sleeped in a good mines. It is a best place we have. After noon today after we walk 6 miles we will divide and go solo 3 days. We get a little food solo, I can eat this food for meal but I have to eat for 3 days, I think I will be hungry. I don't care hungry because I was hungry 6 months on my ship."

On the fifteenth day of his trip, Mai writes about the refugees on the ship and notes, "...3 days don't eat I was hungry too but if I think about my peoples the refugee they are going on a see, they don't know when they get food, when they get a land, they are hungry a lots than me..."

Mai's writing skills were not the best, but remember, he was learning on his own through a "crash course," while attending an American high school in Fort Collins, Colorado. The point of sharing his diary passages is to illustrate his emotions and the pain he still held inside him. Somehow, he has maintained his resiliency, and he knows how to look forward and learn from his experiences.

Next stop?

his or her daily ration). Even with this small amount of food, motion sickness occurred, and it was tough to hold down what little food we consumed. This was only one of the many life-changing effects we would experience. We knew what life was like before and after

Communism and now, as fleeing refugees on this ship. What was next? How would we survive if we reached Hong Kong? Would we ever experience the American culture or dream?

The long and harrowing ship ride had lasting memories—and not necessarily good ones.

7

The Hong Kong Docking

From the Philippines to where? I did not know where we were heading, but trusted we were headed for the land of freedom. Rumor said Hong Kong was our next direct stop. The entire boat trip was twenty-one days from Vietnam to Hong Kong. Naturally, I wouldn't know that until we arrived. Having been chased out of the Philippines, I didn't know if we would be accepted at the next stop. How does a person deal with this kind of rejection?

I suppose one can view this rejection as positive in the sense there was hope for what would happen next. On the other hand, it certainly could have worried me about whether I would ever land, much less in a place where I could be free. From my perspective, one chooses his or her response—you can choose the positive view or you can choose the negative view.

To avoid internalizing rejection, we must choose to face our fears and share our experience, no matter how shameful. To do so mini-

Here is where I think Mai views this journey as an experience and not a personal attack against his heritage or condition. His choice is to discount the rejection and search for a successful outcome. The lesson is not to let rejection color the concept of what we are, but to learn from it and then let it go. There is an old saying I'll paraphrase: If we keep looking in the rearview mirror, we will miss what is ahead of us.

mizes our loneliness. As we face our fears and share the emotions of our experience, we are sure to encounter others with similar stories... perhaps worse ones. This is vital in turning the tide of rejection. Suddenly, your focus shifts from you and the things you might or might not have done to the knowledge that rejection is just an experience like any other negative experience.

I believed all along that the intended destination of the ship with its cargo was Hong Kong. This particular ship's final destination was Hong Kong, so it was not surprising to the Coast Guard to see the ship coming into the coastal area. As the *Skyluck* floated in close to Hong Kong, everyone hid from view of the Coast Guard. To hide approximately twenty-seven hundred people onboard, we had to crowd and push people out of sight, all within limited space on the ship. There was a profound silence, as we approached. Everyone wondered if we would be accepted. Only the crackling of the ship and the waves against the bow could be heard over the noise of the *Skyluck*'s engines.

When the *Skyluck* arrived, people cheered, anticipating they were about to embark in a free country. In Mai's exact expressions, *"the feeling that you no longer have any fear, because we are in a free country. ... We feel like we were re-born. ... A feeling of being safe... traveling for twenty-one days at sea, but now actually see humans on the other side of the water. I remember everyone getting out on the top level of the ship, leaning over the top balcony, the ship leaned to one*

Photograph taken and provided by Mr. Chan Kiu in Hong Kong, who is now living in Vancouver, Canada

side because of so many people—they were afraid the ship was going to tip over...everyone started yelling to get back so the ship wouldn't tip." There was clamoring, as relief and happiness now seemed to be the order of the day. You can imagine how our hearts were filled with joy—this had been a long and difficult journey.

Arriving early in the morning, we saw the Coast Guard approaching with food. We felt welcomed! My sister and I, along with everyone else, felt free and glad to be at our final destination. What a successful experience—now, the nightmare was over!

By that same afternoon, we received more rice in a bigger portion this time. It was accompanied by some cooked chicken with two pieces of white bread, one-quarter piece of orange, one-quarter of a can of beans, a quart of condensed milk, and a quarter can of ham, all to last for two days.

Then, the news came. On the day we arrived, the Hong Kong Coast Guard told us that we could not be brought to shore yet.

In Mai's exact words: *"...at that time we completely trusted the Hong Kong government... everybody was upbeat and we were so happy that everyone arrived to a free country and that soon after that we could start a new life...so everyone is happy and willing to wait and be patient with the Hong Kong government to get us on land."*

However, the heartbreaking news that there was no room for twenty-seven hundred refugees (five hundred were dropped off in the Philippines before the ship was chased away) gave us a sinking feeling.

Yes, another rejection. Nevertheless, the people on the *Skyluck* held onto their hope. We thought that perhaps the Hong Kong government might change its mind after a week or so. We kept our eyes on the prize; we were not willing to give up so fast.

Days, then weeks, went by without a response. We were being held at bay with nowhere to go. People were getting ill and becoming very weary, feeling broken and destitute. How long should we, as a community on the ship, wait before taking another course of action? Leadership and decisions were needed. From the drama and necessity of the *Skyluck* community circumstance, leaders emerged. Our stories were heartbreaking; yet the faith and determination— the *spirit* of all these boat people—showed how mountains can be moved and goals achieved in the face of extreme hardship.

Keep in mind, February was not good weather for everyone to relax and enjoy the sunshine. In my diary, it says, *"We got to make do with what we have. It was cold at night...we had no choice but to tough it out. At night, we went down into the 'paper cave'* [where the

Skyluck stored their spools of paper for delivery]...*that's where we slept, between the floors. Everyone literally slept next to each other, like fish in a can, like sardines in a can, right next to each other.*" The sea waves moved the ship occasionally, reminding us where we were, temporarily. We were still upbeat

> *I like what Thomas Edison told the media when they accused him of failed light bulb experiments. He said, "I have not failed. I've just found 10,000 ways that won't work." Now, Mai and his shipmates had to find something that would work.*

because we had arrived at a free country, which was a big deal... that's what we wanted.

With many nighttime conversations, I could hear most people talking about their plans and the things they wanted to accomplish in their new lives. Many talked about friends in the United States and reuniting with family members they had not seen in years. "*It was a positive environment.*" Most people expressed hope, not despair.

My sister and I did not think differently of ourselves, based on the possessions we carried in relation to the others. Some refugees carried more clothing, and others brought money with them. We just accepted the conditions that we had; we didn't complain. At this time, it was enough just to survive and move on. I don't think we ever felt sorry for ourselves with the conditions we had.

Nevertheless, we, as ship-riders, understood that we must try something new and different to continue the journey.

8

The Hunger Strike

Two or three months later, sitting on the ship in the Hong Kong harbor, Thu-Hong and I realized that nothing was improving or changing to get us on land. The spokespeople were voicing concern to the Hong Kong government. We were at the mercy of those still living on the *Skyluck*.

After the trip to the Philippines, the Vietnamese took over the leadership on the *Skyluck*. South Vietnamese military people living on the same ship as freedom seekers eventually took command of the ship, mainly because they outnumbered all other groups. Action was needed to change the stagnant situation and the government's rebuff of the refugees. These people needed a way to influence officials, but from where was that to come? The only leverage we had was the threat of twenty-seven hundred Vietnamese on the ship. The shipmates didn't campaign or formally vote to determine who would provide leadership for the group. There was no official announcement. Everyone

I often think that companies have discord within their organizations because they lack a genuine mission—not just a written mission statement on a plaque or banner, but a mission to which employees are committed—for which they understand that the company's survival depends on their actions. What I have noticed is that, without a real mission, employees bicker over petty things—technicalities, working conditions, hostile work environments, harassment allegations, and self-serving issues. Of course, this doesn't negate the fact that some of these complaints are valid, but many of these issues would certainly decrease with a genuine and specific direction with attainable, quantifiable goals.

You will see how organized and well managed these 'boat people' survivalists were, yet none attended a leadership conference or took college courses. They were self-taught. Their first real-life lesson and test was their hunger strike.

just understood who or what group was in charge. All the communication throughout the ship was by word of mouth. Daily rumors were rampant about what was going to happen next.

Once the ship leaders realized that no response was coming from the Hong Kong government, they decided to go on a hunger strike. Everyone supported the hunger strike. All knew that this was a team effort, and it was important for each person to participate. There was a consensus!

The usual process of feeding the people on the *Skyluck* was structured and well organized. The Hong Kong military normally brought the food out to us by a floating platform that docked with the ship. This floating platform served as our trading dock. Another ship brought the daily food to the platform for the Vietnamese leaders to collect, sort out, and distribute to all of us onboard.

There were unwritten but understood policies and rules of behavior on the ship. Parked about fifty yards from the refugee ship was a Hong Kong Coast Guard ship standing watch 24/7. Additionally, the Coast Guard posted four to five guards on the *Skyluck* for an extra set of eyes. There was no need for the guards to feel intimidated. The behavior of the people on the ship was amazingly calm. I never saw anyone fighting on the ship. Perhaps some were frustrated and felt anger from time to time, but no one ever erupted.

Daily operations on the ship seemed to take on some sort of instinctive organization—a community within the ship that knew how to carry on with very little chaos or pandemonium. Even though these people came from different towns—from various cultures within Vietnam and of all ages—we knew how to pull together as one society for the sole purpose of survival and to endure. Everyone had a mission!

The hunger strike was planned about two weeks in advance, so we could store food for the kids and elderly. Knowing it could take a while to send our message and influence Hong Kong, we prepared for the worst-case scenario. The young and the elderly were always highly regarded and protected. Additionally, we didn't want to deal with illnesses caused by hunger.

When the strike started, no memorandum was sent out to each person. When food was delivered to the floating dock, no one picked up any products. The Hong Kong government continued to bring food and stockpiled it on the floating dock for seven days.

After seven days, we realized that the government didn't care. The older people and kids started getting sick. So, we started accepting food again. During one of the feedings, many people got food poisoning. Thu-Hong was so ill that she was taken ashore to the hospital. I didn't know she was taken, and I went looking for her. I feverishly looked around the ship deck and in the infirmary area for her, with

When Winston Churchill spoke before his old high school, Harrow School in England, on October 29, 1941, he stated in his speech, "Never give in. Never give in. Never, never, never, never--in nothing, great or small, large or petty--never give in, except to convictions of honor and good sense. Never yield to force. Never yield to the apparently overwhelming might of the enemy... Do not let us speak of darker days; let us speak rather of sterner days. These are not dark days; these are great days--the greatest days our country has ever lived; and we must all thank God that we have been allowed, each of us according to our stations, to play a part in making these days memorable in the history of our race."

Mai has never been a quitter or willing to give in to the appearance of problems, even if they looked dismal with no solution in sight. The dark days only meant there must be light somewhere.

no luck. While peaking inside the infirmary, the ship tipped, and I fell forward. Another person standing nearby caught me, thinking that I fainted and carried me into the infirmary. Suddenly, I realized that the people in the infirmary were waiting to be van transferred to the onshore hospital in Hong Kong. So, I chose to remain there, hoping to find Thu-Hong.

That evening, I was taken off the ship, and I spent the night in the hospital. The next morning, I took my first bath in five months. I went back to the hospital bed, and a doctor approached and tried to talk with me. There was a language barrier, and we couldn't understand each other. The doctor became irritated and started screaming at me. I suddenly experienced my first taste of discrimination and the way people treat you differently because of your culture. I noticed this same doctor treated the Chinese people in the adjacent bed very kindly.

Perhaps it was a rich-man/poor-man syndrome of treatment, but either way, it was a form of discrimination from my perspective.

I was frustrated with not finding Thu-Hong, even after looking around the hospital for her. However, two days later, I discovered that she was back on the ship after being treated in the hospital— leaving the hospital before I arrived there.

This journey seemed like a never-ending fight to survive, but no one would yield to defeat. It was a never-ending drive to come up with more ideas of how we could achieve a permanent landing.

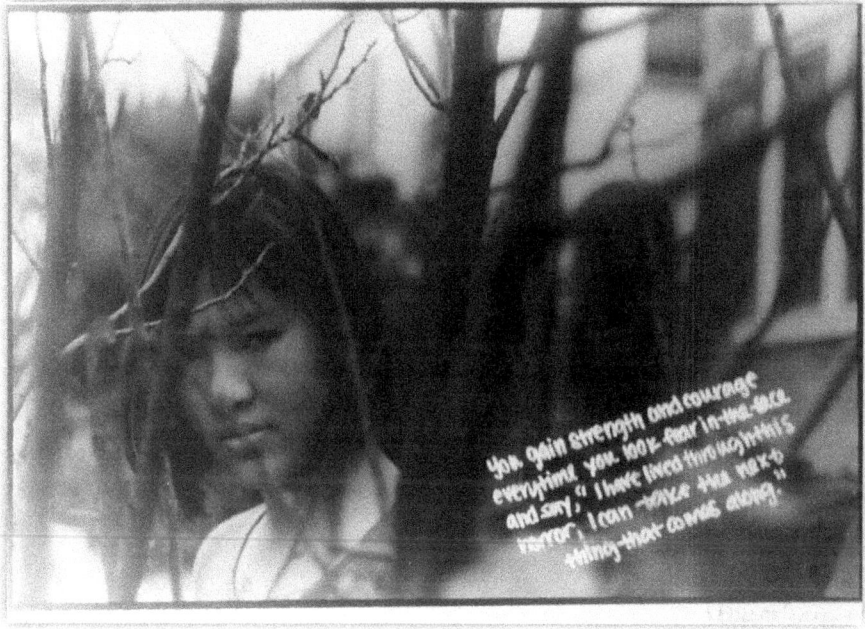

Mai's youngest daughter, Melissa, illustrates the intestinal fortitude she learned from her father's ordeal in a portrait she took of herself. Inscribed on the photograph, she writes, "You gain strength and courage every time you look fear in the face and say, 'I have lived through this horror; I can take the next that comes along.'"

9

The Big Swim

The leadership on the *Skyluck* was not willing to stop generating ideas—their minds were turning constantly. What else was there to do? They decided that their next plan of action would be to organize a group of people to swim to shore, which was three to four miles away.

The initiative was that the swimmers would carry a letter to shore and sneak it to the media to alert the world how we were being treated. Three hundred people volunteered to be swimmers, and all we needed was one person to make it to shore and find the local newspaper. We were desperate to communicate to the world, and signs were placed on the side of the *Skyluck* but attracted little attention. Signs were draped on the sides of the ship saying, "Let us land please we are lonely, come to see us daily, please" and "Food & Medicine, Save Refugees' lives!!" People held high a white banner with "Please Help Us" written in red. Intentionally, most of these signs were written in English.

This was a long swim, and plenty of preparation was made to assure someone would make it. Yes, I was one of the volunteer swimmers. Others helped the swimmers by saving and sharing their food with us, so we, the swimmers, could be stronger to swim. Here again, everyone was part of the mission and helped in even the smallest way. We prepared five-gallon tins to use as flotation devices and as a place to store the letters inside for delivery to the media. Many duplicate letters were prepared, so each swimmer had one—no one knew who would make it. The tension was building, and the anxiety in us to get it done was driving a sense of determination and urgency.

Our next concern was when and where we would dive into the ocean without the Coast Guard knowing, especially the guards posted on the ship. It would take another community gathering to create a distraction. The morning of the swim, the leaders organized a fake fight at the back of the ship that drew all the guards—including the Coast Guard ship—to the organized fight. This staged disturbance worked perfectly as a diversion.

Meanwhile, we swimmers slipped to the other end of the ship and methodically launched our flight to freedom. Three hundred swimmers jumped in, including me. When I hit the water, I was shocked, and I realized it was too cold for me to make the swim—I retreated immediately. Only about one hundred and fifty people eventually took the swim challenge—the rest retreated. No one expected that the force of swimmers would be cut in half; but remember that we only needed one to succeed. I was disappointed that I couldn't make the swim, yet reluctantly yielded to my known limitations. Knowing your limitations is key to *survival*, not just success.

Once the Coast Guard realized what was happening, they quickly maneuvered their ship to block the swimmers. This served two purposes: they blocked the swimmers and rescued those swimmers who would have obviously drowned. Those people were promptly returned to the ship.

About thirty people made it to shore. However, the police were already waiting for them, and they were subsequently arrested. Nevertheless, rumors were rampant that one person got through and supposedly went directly into Hong Kong by ferry. This person knew how to speak Chinese, managed to find his way to a local newspaper outlet, and delivered the letter. We learned that the messenger was eventually arrested because local people turned him in, knowing he wasn't a resident because of his dress and behavior. He was returned to the ship about one week later, telling everyone his story that verified the initial rumors. Miraculously, during this whole ordeal, only one person drowned.

I think that, after the attempted swim, the Hong Kong Coast Guard pulled their security team off the ship, realizing that it wasn't preventing the refugees from attempting to escape. There were never any disruptions or need for policing on the ship. The *Skyluck* community knew how to get along, living peaceably and learning to work with each other for a single cause—survival.

10

Cutting all Anchors

Something had to be done! We were back to the drawing board, yet still driven to get on land. After a month of contemplating our next step, everyone agreed to sink or swim. The next plan we came up with was to cut the ship's anchor and drift to shore. The leaders of the refugees on the ship worked for another month on the idea and ways to implement this plan.

We knew when the anchor was cut, the Coast Guard would push the ship back out to sea. So, to prevent this from happening, we prepared mini-Molotov cocktails out of small baby food jars. The idea was that when the Coast Guard ship attempted to push us away from the land, we would throw the miniature firebombs at the Coast Guard ship to divert their attention,—the Coast Guard would focus on extinguishing their fires, rather than pushing the *Skyluck* back out to sea. We prepared many of these Molotov cocktails.

The next scheme, if everything else went as planned, was for hundreds of people to jump off the ship and swim to shore, once again distracting the Coast Guard away from the people on the ship, particularly the young and the elderly. As the ship drifted toward land during these distractions, everyone was hopeful that, if the ship were close enough to shore, the children and the elderly could use the ship's stairs to disembark.

At the same time, those who jumped and swam to shore would run from the guard to draw a foot chase, knowing that the runners wouldn't be shot. Once the guards were close enough, or they saw enough of the guards chasing them, the running refugees agreed to yield by sitting down right away. This would attract most of the guards while those who remained on the ship could disembark and fade quietly out of sight. The ship had stairs that could reach the water, but many people still needed assistance with swimming a short distance because of their youth, elderliness, health conditions, or disabilities.

The final stage of this plan, once the elderly, kids, and disabled people were safely moved from the ship onto land, was to puncture a hole in the ship and sink it. We didn't want the ship rendered safe for reboarding or remaining intact to be forced back out to sea.

We all viewed this as our last ditch effort. We felt we had reached a point of no return—either sink or swim. When we left Vietnam, the idea of a point of no return started in Binh Dai, the town my sister and I left to reach the first vessel. I replicated this same lesson when making my commitment to starting my own business—it was a sense of no return and a commitment for success. In my mind, failure was not an option. If we had failed to reach shore, my family wouldn't be here now. Sometimes, we have to sink our own ship to succeed—or at least to get rid of the anchors holding us back.

Now came the time to execute our plan. It seemed as if everything was falling in sync, just as intended. People knew what their positions were; who was to jump, throw firebombs, cut the anchor, and start tearing a hole in the ship's bowels; and who was to lead the escape down the ship's stairs and help the kids and elderly swim ashore. Timing was everything, and what might have seemed chaotic from the outside looking in was very well orchestrated from within. The anxiety was different, as we had been through so many other failed attempts; there was much anticipation of succeeding. We knew that something had to give, one way or another, if everyone executed his or her job well. This was it! We were out of options and determined to make this work.

Ironically, everything planned was executed perfectly and as expected. The anchor was cut, and when the Coast Guard saw the *Skyluck* floating inward, they started to push the ship back out to sea. When this pushing started, the fueled baby jars were hurled at the Coast Guard, causing them to back away and tend to their own fire. Once again, we were drifting inland, and when the ship got close enough, hundreds of people jumped overboard, drawing the guards to chase them and give up pushing the *Skyluck* back out to sea. While the shore police and guard chased the divers, this allowed ample time to start unloading the elderly and children along with any disabled refugees. With precision timing, another team of refugees began tearing a hole in the boat to sink it after everyone had safely exited the ship.

When the Coast Guard realized they had lost control, they asked the people to stop jumping and trying to leave the ship, which was becoming chaotic. They agreed to help them come ashore orderly and safely. The *Skyluck* was sinking miserably, and the Coast Guard knew they couldn't push it back out to sea; they knew the anchors were cut loose and that it was futile to do anything to save the ship. One can see the picture of the sinking *Skyluck* at http://www.library. ubc.ca/asian/FinalAsian/Vietnam/V-16.html along with many other photographs.

Those making it to shore were taken to the Lamma Island police post. Even after their capture and detention, they posted a sign pressed against the wired prison fence saying, "please help us." This image is captured in a Web site photograph at *www.library.ubc.ca/ asian/FinalAsian/Vietnam/V-12.html* along with many other photographs.

I was convinced that everyone had the attitude that "No doubt—we are going to reach land" or "We had to do it, regardless of the outcome!"

Little did they know that confinement was imminent on this new island.

Photographs taken and provided by Mr. Chan Kiu in Hong Kong, who is now living in Vancouver, Canada"

The Skyluck ship's last stand

11

Lockdown

The *Skyluck* ran out of luck.

It sank, and all its passengers were on shore. I was ready to take the next step in my journey for freedom, theorizing that I wouldn't stay in Hong Kong, but probably move on to another country. The next thing we knew, we all were being loaded on a ferry the same afternoon we got off the sunken ship. Everybody assumed that we were headed to a refugee camp.

Arriving at night on an unknown island, everyone lined up. For what? To be sprayed with some kind of chemical, probably for lice or other types of possible contagious infections. This made me feel like a dog and as if we were being treated like animals. I was sprayed from head to toe with my clothes on. The women and men were separated and were paraded to their respective barracks. While walking to the barracks, I noticed that the barracks were enclosed with chain-linked fence and barbed wire at the top.

Suddenly, I realized we were in a *prison* camp. There were bars on the windows, and once inside, I could hear the eeriness of the front door slam shut and lock—the sound of a padlock from the outside. Each person picked his or her own bed. It was unquestionably crowded with about one hundred and fifty people in the barracks. The floor was laid out with bunk beds on each side of the wall with about a two-foot walkway to pass down the aisle. Even though the place projected the image of a prison, the environment was nonetheless a step up for us, considering our squalid living conditions on the ship.

I guess Mai sees the glass as half full instead of half empty. For a 16-year-old boy to view this circumstance as he did is amazing. To stare at bars on windows, be surrounded by wire fence walls, to hear doors lock behind you, and to lie down in a small cot and say, "This is a step up" is remarkable. One can only imagine what it was like to have survived the harsh conditions on the ship for six months.

The first night was quiet; no one talked, because he or she was exhausted. When I went to bed, I couldn't help but reflect on the journey and realize our significant accomplishment thus far. It would have been easy for a person to feel doomed; however, considering what little we had at the beginning of the journey, how could this particular stop be a failure? After all, I was in a bed, or rather, a military-type cot.

Early the next morning, the guards woke everyone and looked for volunteers for various tasks. I knew the saying, "If you want to eat, you have to be in the kitchen." My survival thinking seemed intuitive—I was always thinking about success and taking the next step. Without a second thought, I quickly volunteered to be a cook. For me to work in the kitchen, the guards cut my hair. Once in the kitchen, I noticed giant-size woks, with industrial-size cooking equipment—it looked like a giant's kitchen to me. When I realized the jackpot I had hit, I began eating the oranges in a nearby box. I remember eating at least twenty oranges in one sitting. When I looked around, everyone in the kitchen was eating something. My main job was cooking rice.

I was worried about my younger sister and other friends. I constantly looked out for them while serving food to others. When I spotted my sister coming through the line, it was like a breath of fresh air to know that she was fine. While I served food in the line and saw Thu-Hong coming through the line, I would place my sister's favorite food in the bottom of her bowl and cover it with rice—a special meal for my sister every day. At night, while walking back to the barracks, I would sneak fruit and other assorted favorite treats to her in the barracks. Despite my physical separation from Thu-Hong, we still maintained our family ties deep within. I knew that, as the older brother, I was responsible for caring for her and watching over my sister's survival. Thu-Hong was so young at this time that I was constantly concerned about her living conditions, whereabouts, and nutritional needs.

After three weeks of working in the kitchen, I got the boot once they found out I was under eighteen years old. So, I volunteered for other jobs to explore more of the outside world around me. I had become weary of working in the kitchen anyway, having to report directly back to the barracks and placed in lockdown right after work each night. We were allowed outdoors for two hours a day, but not beyond the camp's fenced walls. I was able to get outside the fence as part of a crew volunteering to do perimeter clean-up work. Even though guards accompanied me, it was a time I sensed freedom—another gauge of success.

I knew it was just a matter of time before the United Nations would intervene and investigate what was happening. The news was out, and Hong Kong couldn't suppress it from the rest of the world. I just had to keep the faith.

12

The U.N. Rescue

As expected, the day came when United Nations' representatives visited our prison camp. It happened during our second month of confinement. They must have felt compelled to check out the situation, given the news media reports. United Nations representatives immediately began interviewing the refugees. The questioning seemed archaic, but it was another step toward freedom. I wondered why they were asking about American POWs. I knew that the U.S. was trying to find soldiers who were missing in action, but I couldn't understand what the MIAs had to do with our plight. Many questions were asked about if we had seen any Americans or American graves in Vietnam. One refugee claimed that he saw American graves—he was immediately removed from the camp area and taken away for further questioning. Each interview lasted about fifteen minutes—it seemed as if they were there for weeks doing interviews.

After the interviews, people were processed into the United Nations refugee camp in Kowlung (one of Hong Kong's islands). The site we were moved to was like an old hotel or apartment building. After staying in prison for four months, I was finally transferred to Kowlung.

Kowlung was a big improvement with more freedoms. The transfer was almost like coming from the dark side to the light of life. My shared room was 10' x 15' in dimension, furnished with six beds, and occupied by ten people. The name of the camp was Jubilee. Camp Jubilee was located in Lai Chi Kok, which housed thousands of refugees. In the 1970s, the YMCA supported the Vietnamese refugee camps in Hong Kong called the Silver Jubilee Centre. was All the refugees were given one week of food, one box per day, and then they were on their own to find their own means of support. Kowlung was like a regular city, and everyone was at liberty to leave the camp to find a job.

While I was talking with Mai, he could still recall and repeat the same phrases—he never forgot; after all, they were his survival tools.

After two or three days at Camp Jubilee, I found a friend who knew how to speak Chinese. He helped translate certain phrases, so I could ask questions such as "Do you need people to work here?" and "How much does it pay per day?"

During my first day of job hunting, I went to a shipyard to haul cases of old wooden boxes of soda from the ship to the ground. I didn't take the job once I saw how hard the labor was. You have to understand that I wasn't used to hard work. My family always had had servants in their household for each child. We didn't do hard work—nothing, just eat and go out, no chores or anything.

While continuing to walk through town, looking for another kind of work, I found a sweater factory and took the job of quality control, checking for defects in the final products. This wasn't a tough job. The manager knew that I didn't have any money, so he took me out for lunch that day. Only earning about five dollars a day, I was frugal and didn't spend money, knowing I had to keep it for food. The next day, I got on the bus to go back to work, but I couldn't find the sweater factory—I was disorientated from the day before and so much walking around. Two hours later, I found the sweater factory and did some fast talking to the manager about why I was late. They seemed to understand my circumstances. The manager was especially nice to me because he didn't have a son, only daughters. This manager, whose name I've forgotten, helped me learn the Chinese language. Part of the reason I don't remember the manager's name is because in the Asian culture, it is improper to call older people by their given name. You can call them "uncle," which is how I referred to him many times.

Three weeks later, I found another job paying twice as much salary. I learned how to make plastic leaves for artificial plants. My previous boss was fine with my taking on the new job as leaf maker. During the first couple of days of working with the leaf-making machine, it broke down. When the mechanic came over to help me, he told me to take the machine apart. I did and literally pulled the entire machine apart. That wasn't what the mechanic wanted. He requested that only a certain part of the machine be dismantled. When the mechanic returned, he was angry about what I had done. He chewed me out, yelling and screaming. My work there ended after one month.

While living at this camp, I also picked up some vices. I learned how to smoke and drink, which is something I would never have done at home. My hair had grown down to my shoulders because that was the style back then.

During this time, my sister, Thu-Hong, contacted a friend in Boulder, Colorado, who had been a neighbor and friend in Vietnam and who had escaped in 1975. She asked the friend to sponsor us to the United States. She filed for sponsorship papers on our behalf. The next thing we knew, we were on a posted list to go to the United States. An American who spoke fluent Vietnamese interviewed both of us again, separately. I assumed this interviewer was CIA, but who knows if that was true or not.

While being interviewed, we were asked where our parents were from, what our parents did before and after 1975, and why we wanted to come to the United States. Once again, the interviewers probed to ascertain if we saw any Americans or POWs in Vietnam. It was a short interview, perhaps fifteen minutes. Two weeks later, we were on our way to the United States. The only reason we were designated for the United States was that the United States was the only country accepting minors (people under the age of eighteen).

13

The Land of the Free

Yes, Thu-Hong and I were U.S.A. bound, but we had to find our own means of transportation to the airport in Hong Kong. We managed, and yet my mind was racing with thoughts of what else could hold us back—it didn't seem as if anything could stop us now. As we arrived at the airport and found ourselves climbing on the airplane, my imagination raced with thoughts of success and wonder about what it would be like in the U.S.A. This was real; our feet planted on the airplane assured me that there was no return to unnecessary pain and suffering, such as no food to eat or wondering where we were going to sleep. Once we were on the airplane, the only thing on my mind was to do what our parents instructed—learn the language and go to school.

The flight was remarkable in the sense that we knew that freedom was just hours away. After landing in Seattle, Washington, on January 9, 1980, the USCC (United States Catholic Charities) helped place us. Thu-Hong and I were escorted through U.S. Customs, and the next thing we knew, we were on our way to Denver as our final destination. I find it ironic that we left Vietnam on January 9, 1979, and arrived in the United States exactly one year later.

Mai reflects on this "moment of truth" in his Outward Bound diary on June 22, 1980, noting: "In camp Hong Kong we tried to go USA, we knew we can go to more and my parents they wanted we do that too. When I came Denver we didn't have some body pick us up, we don't be afrait, we don't scare but I was sad. I didn't know how we live and where do we stay."

Keep in mind, Mai is writing this diary for his foster mother during his camping trip. In this diary, Mai attempts to solidify his personal relationship with his new foster mother. Conveying the need for family and the need to be loved by others, he writes, "The first time I met you, I like you...I think you com help us. How it is right, you try to help us very

The plan was to meet with the family of Thu-Hong's friend at the airport. However, no one showed up! We wandered around the old Stapleton Airport terminal in Denver for six hours, not knowing the language or a place to meet anyone.

Finally, we met a Vietnamese woman, Thuy, at the airport—she worked for the Lutheran Church helping other Vietnamese refugees. It was obvious to Thuy that we were refugees—we carried a cardboard sign with our names and birthdates displayed. Someone from Catholic Charities prepared the display board and information for us.

It was surprisingly refreshing to hear Thuy speak our language. Thuy offered to take both of us to her home, and of course, we agreed. We stayed with her the first night, along with Thuy's two kids, one age six and the other about age eight at the time—Thuy was a single mom. The next morning when Thuy left for work with the kids, we cleaned her house for her to show our gratefulness.

Thuy called USCC to let them know we were in her custody, so we would not accidentally be listed as missing. That night when she came home from work, she visited with both of us and offered to be our sponsor. Thuy's generosity came about when she discovered that our previous sponsors, the friends of Thu-Hong, had dropped their sponsorship without notice. We readily and gladly accepted Thuy's offer. However, Catholic Charities refused Thuy's offer and demanded that we be removed from her home immediately. Catholic Charities claimed responsibility for both of us. Thuy was left without a choice, and she sadly relinquished us the next day to representatives of Catholic Charities.

We were taken to the Denver church office wondering what was going to happen next. We met a Vietnamese man who worked for the USCC who asked us what we wanted to do when we settled into a home. I spoke up and explained our objectives, yet he seemed very negative regarding our capabilities and suggested that we find a job instead of going to school. This Vietnamese counselor even used the analogy of his own son not being able to complete school and attend college—noting that his son spoke fluent English. He really demoralized us in a threatening way. Thu-Hong and I were on the

much. I don't know how to say thank you. We need famille and you gave us famille. Some body think us need food, they are wrong, we need some body love and like us, we didn't have it in camp, now you are giving for us all this. You understand us... look like my mother. I want to live with you all my life I don't want to leave you any more...I love you I like you very much, I look you same my mother. All the sentences I wrote it's my mind, but I want to know how do you think about us...I am stronger than I lived with my parents because I have TH my younger sitter. ... she doesn't know not thing...I have to help and guardian her. 2 years ago we look like baby birds can't fly in a big sky...six months we lived on a ship."

same page, though, and had similar thoughts about this man: "Your son must really be dumb." More than ever, we were determined to succeed.

The next step was being transferred to a temporary housing site with other refugees, where we met a supervisor named David. He was very courteous to us, even taking us shopping with him. One week later, we were placed with foster parents Marty and Jim Dwyer from Fort Collins, Colorado, some miles north of Denver. The Dwyers took us under their wing and helped us as much as possible.

14

Our Foster Home

Marty and Jim Dwyer met Thu-Hong and me in Denver, driving up in a big station wagon with their ten-month-old son, Dennis, and a translator, Huong, from Colorado State University (in Fort Collins). The ride back with them was somewhat quiet while we listened to everyone talking in English. Looking at the highway, I-25 seemed empty, with very little traffic compared to Vietnam and Hong Kong. We felt as if we were going to some small village because of what we perceived as too few vehicles.

However, it didn't really matter to us. This was another step forward—it didn't make any difference at this point whom we were with, knowing we were probably going to attend school.

When we arrived at Marty and

Humorously, Mai noted that one of the first sayings he learned was "beggars can't be choosers," and that's the way he saw life in America. He was determined to make the best of any situation in which he was placed.

Jim's home, we discovered five additional sons in the Dwyer family. We were introduced and shown where to sleep for the night—I had a small bed in the laundry room, while my sister stayed alone in a room next to the laundry room. Because of the unknown American culture, Thu-Hong was afraid to stay in her room alone. Consequently, I moved my bed into the same room with her. I sensed that the middle son, Kevin (age fourteen), wasn't really accepting us yet. However, Chris, who was ten years old at the time, came to our room and tried to talk with us. Even though we couldn't understand each other's words, I knew that younger Chris was making us feel welcomed.

When I asked Mai if he had been confident that he would learn the language, he replied: "It wasn't confidence that I had; I just knew we would do it, because we had to move forward—we just had to do it."

The next day, we were taken to school to watch a basketball game to experience an American sport. However, we were uncomfortable from jetlag, and we were finding it very hard to adjust to American food, eating only tidbits of food to get by because we didn't initially like the taste of school food. It was also difficult to evaluate the school culture because of the sudden social change.

One week later, right after New Year's Day, I enrolled in Fort Collins High School, and my sister was signed up to attend Boltz Junior High School. My first day in school was an abrupt challenge. Without any interpreters, I was given a math test to determine into what level I should be placed. I recognized the math symbols, which are almost the same as in the Vietnamese schools, with the exception of the comma and the period—their definitions and their use are *reversed* in Vietnam. Obviously, I flunked every test they gave me, and I was placed in very basic level math. Of course, I didn't understand a word anyone said, so I didn't know how well I tested—I just went home assuming all was well. From then on, I attended school with my foster brother, Jimmy. While riding on the bus, no one talked to me for obvious reasons. I frequently sat in the bus seat alone watching everyone else engaged in various conversations, feeling very disconnected.

I signed up for various classes—math, French, chemistry, and so on. The school provided a special teacher to help me with English for one hour per day. She also spoke French, which I understood and which helped with our translation issues. I didn't question the teacher's inability to speak Vietnamese but learned through her pointing to pictures and having me repeat the names of objects I saw.

It took me about three months to have a decent grasp of the English language—to read and write efficiently and converse with people. My mastery of the English language wasn't efficient enough to convey personal feelings, but only efficient enough to navigate basic needs.

I related to much of what Mai was talking about as we teach our kids at home to identify and repeat the names of objects as well. Mai smiled when he reflected on how it would take him hours to read one page of text using the English and French dictionaries. Why French? While in Vietnam, his parents put him through French classes. He learned to write in French before he learned to write in Vietnamese. Mai had a general grasp of speaking different languages, such as Vietnamese, Thai, French, and Cantonese, when he came to the United States.

I was enrolled into a summer program called Outward Bound for a three-week camping trip in the Silverton/Durango area in the Colorado Rockies. I didn't know it was going to entail long hiking trips of ten to fifteen miles per day and carrying all your own gear and food (this was a surprise survival crash course for me). I wrote a complete diary of my excruciating trip and gave it to my foster mother. She kept it for many years and asked me to take it back before she passed away in 2005. My original writing about this Outward Bound trip can be found in Appendix A of this book.

When I asked him why he didn't pick up his diary before she died, he stated, "I didn't want to face the fact that she was dying." He didn't feel comfortable retrieving his diary that he had given as a gift to his foster mother. Mai noted that the only funeral he ever attended was his foster mother's burial—he's not a fan of funerals and avoids them. Amazingly, Mai wrote his Outward Bound trip diary after being in the United States for only six months—his sophomore year in school.

During my junior year in high school, I still struggled with English. I participated in a few events in school, such as school assemblies, but I never felt I was part of the school or of any social crowd. School dances or sporting events weren't for me—not because I wasn't interested—I had a different mission. My *job* was to attend school and work—that was my mindset. I also held three outside jobs while attending school.

Delivering bundles of newspapers to various newspaper carriers' homes was one of my jobs. Consequently, I was up very early in the morning (1:00 a.m. until 5:00 a.m. on the weekends) to make these necessary drop-offs.

My second job was working for a professor in the forestry department at CSU as a computer programmer. I learned about programming during my junior year of high school. Professor James Smith and I met during a school field trip to CSU. A counselor introduced me to Mr. Smith, knowing that I was already advanced in math. This was my first introduction to the computer world, and Mr. Smith instructed me in computer programming. I was hired to work with CSU for $5.35 per hour. My third job? At United Daycare Center as a babysitter for school kids (as an assistant). Oh, yes, I had a fourth job on occasion, picking up trash around the high school.

Even though these jobs might seem too humble for students to work around other students or their peers, it didn't matter to me—I had a mission, and it didn't concern me who was watching. My goal was to finish college, and each of these various jobs was another step toward a college education.

It was important for me to take computer classes. Xuan, who worked at HP and who was also from Vietnam and had come to the U.S. in 1975, mentored me. Xuan is now a U.S. citizen. I wanted a stable job, knowing that my profession was going to be a *computer scientist*. During my high school years, I only had one friend—another Vietnamese person by the name of Thanh Tran (no biological relationship). Thanh came to the United States in 1975 on a U.S. Navy ship. Thanh and I had several classes together, shared school notes, and studied together to make it through school.

My life wasn't without some trouble in school. I had difficulty adjusting to the time change and frequently fell asleep in school. I was falling asleep so much that my foster parents took me to a doctor to make sure I was functioning normally. Everything checked out well for me. More than likely, I was still trying to adjust to the pressures of this new country.

On one occasion, I was in the cafeteria for lunch, and a group of five Hispanic students walked by me making some disparaging remarks. I didn't know what they said, but I could tell by their facial expressions, voice inflection, and body language that it wasn't friendly. Ironically, I had a P.E. class with these same guys. When we played soccer together, these same students deliberately pushed me around. The P.E. teacher told me to push them back. With my teacher's advice, I decided not to tolerate it any further. I resorted to my former training in Vietnam where I had learned judo. So, the next time these guys pushed me, I quickly tossed the first guy to the ground. He was the biggest kid, and the rest of them stayed away without further challenge. This same guy tried attacking me a couple more times, to no avail. He left me alone from then on. These guys knew I would defend myself.

Even my P.E. teacher saw some of this interaction and tested my ability, only to find himself on the ground as well. That's when I was recruited for the wrestling team and was awarded a place on the varsity team. However, I quit because of my necessary part-time jobs. Next, they tried to recruit me for football. I looked at the equipment and said, "No way am I going to carry those things and run with them." My sport was soccer. The coaches figured my martial arts knowledge and ability to run fast could be an asset to the team—but not for now; I was too focused on my goal.

> Once again, Mai refers in his Outward Bound diary (June 27, 1980) to how people treated or stereotyped him: "I was very sad, I try to talk with they but I can't, I don't know why? I think because I have black hair, I am not American. They look at me funny, I don't like, I go to sleep soon when they are together. I want to talk with my teacher about that and I tell with him I want to go home…I have only one thing to do, take a pictures, I don't talk, I don't laugh anymore…my god, help me, I try to finish outward bound. I am thinking about my famille in Vietnam. I hope they have a food and they are happy." He continues to write about this concern the next day, stating,

My junior year in high school was progressively improving with new friends and stronger English skills. On occasion, some of my classmates wanted to learn how to cuss in Vietnamese. With my playfulness and sly humor, I taught them how to curse.

While learning English, many times, I didn't realize what I was saying, confusing slang used by students with the literal meaning of those same slang terms. This created confusion and chaos for me. On one occasion, I was talking to a girl that I had made friends with and was trying to say, "I will see you early tomorrow." Instead, I said, "I will see you ugly tomorrow." She looked at me with surprise and a bit of disgust. I couldn't understand why. So, after asking my foster mother about the incident, I got it.

On another occasion, the sister of my foster mother purchased a new condo. So, I, trying to be friendly, greeted her, "Hi, Aunt Peg, how is your condom, do you like it? I'm happy you bought a condom. I want to go over and see it…." While talking, I noticed that Aunt Peg's face became flushed. I knew something was wrong with what I said, so I stopped talking. Without hesitation, I walked away, without realizing that the term I used referred to a contraceptive instead of a place to live, and the conversation quickly changed.

"All the people I knew in Fort Collins, they don't laugh me when I was wrong, they don't look me funny. I loved Fort Collins very much because it has my mom my sittor and all the people I like. I want to cry now but I can't because I didn't cry anymore. I don't want they think Vietnamese soft…the peoples in this country many don't like me because I am refugee, I don't have a house and family…they don't know, I am having a new famille…I don't need the people in my group anymore."

More than likely, Mai picked up the term "see you later ugly" from other students who said it in jest to their friends, but Mai mistook it for proper English.

I took a liking to writing poetry and kept a notebook with all my poetry written in Vietnamese and another notebook with it written in English. I had a special writing talent without realizing it. My foster brother, Jim, noticed that I received an A in creative writing class. Jim thought if I could pass the creative writing class so easily with my limited English, surely he could pass the class with flying colors. After taking the class, Jim discovered it wasn't as easily done—I think he flunked the class. Ironically, Jim is now a writer and has published a couple of books.

> *Mai Tran wrote the following two poems—yet another talent of his that helps him understand the many journeys he has traveled. Mai has written more than one hundred poems but has yet to publish them. These poems are for those who can read Vietnamese. Translation into the English language doesn't have the same expression as the original Vietnamese dialect offers.*

Cho Đến Bao Giờ

Cho đến bao giờ tôi mới trở về

Quê hương đất mẹ tràng trề yêu thương

Cho đến bao giờ tôi mới được nghe

Lời thương triều mến mẹ hiền ru con

Cho đến bao giờ tôi mới được xem

Hàng me xanh thẩm bên đường Duy Tân

Cho đến bao giờ tôi mới được yêu

Yêu cô gái Việt bên bờ sông Hương

Tha Hương

Tha hương một kiếp thăng trầm

Tha hương tôi đến mười lăm năm trường

Khi rời đất mẹ quê hương

Đường đời bỡ ngỡ lòng vương lắm sầu

Những chiều trời   đổ mưa ngâu

Lòng tôi ướt   đẫm nỗi sầu cố hương

Tôi thương tôi mãi còn thương

Đô Thành Cư Xá con   đường me xanh

Bài thơ chiếc nón rộng vành

Thướt tha cô bé tập tành bước yêu

Ai đi tôi gởi những chiều

Mưa trên đất khách vời nhiều nhớ thương

15

Moving Out and Ready for College

My senior year in high school did not change much; I had already moved out from my foster parents' home into an apartment. I moved out of respect for my foster family, who were already raising five boys and Thu-Hong in a four-bedroom home. In addition, I was already holding down three, sometimes four, jobs. Meanwhile, I decided to sponsor my cousin, Hung Phan, to come into the U.S. from the refugee camp in Hong Kong.

When Hung Phan arrived, I needed to be more independent and responsible for my own support. My sister, Thu-Hong, stayed with our foster family. Around the same time that I moved out, my other two sisters, Thu-Van and Thu-Nga, moved into our foster parents' home. Thu-Van and Thu-Nga came from a Philippine refugee camp after they escaped from Vietnam about one year after my escape. I didn't move too far from school; it was a duplex located behind Fort Collins Muffler shop on South College Avenue. Hung Pham took a different path and chose not to attend school. Instead, he worked at the muffler shop near our duplex apartment.

When I graduated from high school, it was just another step in my quest. I wasn't excited to receive a high school diploma, nor did I have any pictures of my graduation or any other celebration. I think that my foster parents might have pictures of me graduating, but I did not keep any for myself. The next step was to attend college and secure a diploma. I didn't apply for admission to college anywhere other than Colorado State University (CSU), located in Fort Collins.

When I asked Mai how Hung Pham learned English, he stated, "You work and learn." Eventually, Hung married a U.S. citizen and worked at the Budweiser plant north of Fort Collins. He and his wife separated, and he subsequently moved to California after living in Fort Collins for twenty years.

Mai has an amazing memory. Some label his ability as a photographic memory. He memorized what was taught in the classroom and whatever he studied from a textbook. Even now, he claims his memorization skill has improved!

In the fall of 1982, I was accepted into CSU. I received some financial aid, along with a small scholarship—I think the scholarship was for $200 to $300. Nevertheless, I was still flying solo, paying for my own rent, food, schooling, and other necessities. College was a breeze, after I learned English; I didn't have to study very hard, and I got good grades. My major was computer science with a minor in math.

Very seldom did I work on homework past 5:00 p.m. During finals week, I met with my sister, Thu-Van, and asked her what she was studying (we frequently took the same classes), and she shared with me. That was all the studying for finals I needed to successfully pass my tests.   Thu-Van was resentful that she had to study so hard, while I was able to comprehend our lessons with little study. Her frustration was actually admiration of my keen skills for comprehension and learning.

Another great success for me was receiving my U.S. citizenship. I applied for citizenship in 1986, and within six months, I took the oral test. Three months later, I was sworn in as a United States citizen.

16

The American Entrepreneur

To celebrate my college graduation, I didn't send the traditional announcements, do the traditional partying, or attend graduation events. I just said good-bye to some of my new friends. Deep down inside, I felt proud and happy and said, "I achieved what my parents wanted me to do." I couldn't notify my parents that I graduated because there was no telephone system in Vietnam. So, I wrote them a letter explaining that I finished school. Letters back then took about one month to arrive. My parents wrote back, congratulating me for my achievement. I started to regain hope that perhaps now, there was a chance for me to bring Dad and Mom to America! I never lost sight of that dream—it would be twelve years after my escape when I would finally reunite with my parents.

*In Mai's own words, "Next step was looking for a job." He searched
for any kind of programming job. After graduating, Mai had two job
offers: Cray Research and Electronic Data Systems (EDS), a company
started by Texas multimillionaire Ross Perot. Mai took the job in
Dallas, Texas, with EDS but suddenly changed his mind when he
received a third job offer with Western Area Power Administration
(WAPA) as a "C" programmer in 1986—right out of college. He stayed
with the company for ten years.*

*During 1988, Mai became friends with Bruce Hottman, another
employee at WAPA who was also a computer programmer. Bruce and
Mai knew that the government contract they were working on was
ending in 1996. They joined forces to analyze the possibility of starting
their own company. They did, and now, it is ITX.*

*Mai and Bruce carefully mapped out the objectives of their potential
company, starting with what service they wanted to provide and what
qualified personnel they needed. It was natural for them to want to
hire experts, not beginners—experts with years of experience. They saw
a need to identify themselves as experts. Consequently, they came up
with the company name of Information Technology eXperts, with the
emphasis on the letter "X" to use as part of their logo—ITX.*

*Initially, it was just Mai and Bruce running the business from Mai's
basement. They didn't do any advertising other than "word of mouth"
networking through their memberships in some civic organizations
and business groups, such as Rotary and the Fort Collins Chamber
of Commerce. For planning and outlining networking systems, they
needed a white board. Money was scarce, but they improvised by using
a bath/shower plastic wall surround as their first grease board. Bruce
and Mai managed their outgoing services from the basement, using
Mai's home telephone.*

*Mai's first customers included Hewlett Packard, Rocky Mountain
Generation Co-op, Quick Appliances, Celestica, and Rickars and Rulon
Accounting Company. Although their services grew and improved, they
still provide services to their first and long-term customers. Now, ITX
has about 150 small business customers and 10 major contractors with*

federal and local governments. They employ 140 people to deliver their services and meet customers' demands, which now range from Help Desk support to system administrators, network analysts, software programmers, telecommunication specialists, and security experts. Mai's attention and commitment to quality service are recognized. Some examples of the company's awards and recognitions are listed below.

2004—Top 50 Minority-Owned Businesses, ITX ranked 25th, ColoradoBiz *magazine*

2005—Mercury 100 Fastest-Growing Private Companies, ITX ranked 20th overall and #1 in the technology industry, Northern Colorado Business Report (NCBR)

2006—ITX named USDA's Small Disadvantaged Business (SDB) Contractor of the Year; Mai Tran and Bruce Hottman named SBA-Colorado Small Business Persons of the Year, Small Business Administration; Mercury 100 Fastest-Growing Private Companies, ITX ranked 22nd, Northern Colorado Business Report (NCBR)

2007—Inc. 5,000 List, America's Fasting Growing Private Companies, ITX ranked #2511
Mercury 100 Fastest-Growing Private Companies, ITX ranked 15th, NCBR (Northern Colorado Business Report); *Top 50 Family-Owned Businesses, ITX ranked 27th,* ColoradoBiz

magazine

2008—ITX ranked #3 on USDA's list of 8(a) IT Top 10 Companies; Mai Tran named Top 10 Finalist, Asian Business Leadership Award, USPAACC and Wells Fargo Bank; Winner, Best in Business Awards, Small/Family-Owned Business of the Year, Fort Collins Coloradoan

"Even the company's customers, whom Mai considers more important than the awards, recognize his quality of service, professionalism, and satisfaction." Bill Brayden, <u>Brayden Automation Corp.</u>

"The one-on-one and web meetings you've had with the employees were very positive. The employees appreciate the attention that ITX has given them during the transition. I believe this was one of the best transitions we have ever had." Western Area Power Administration.

"ITX continually exceeds our expectations. Their response time is unbelievable and there is no problem too big or small for them to handle. We would not be able to do our business without them!" Brenda Nickel, Business Manager, The Group, Inc. Real Estate.

"ITX's performance under all the USDA contracts has been exemplary. The performance-based contracts have exceeded the minimum acceptable time and quality performance standards every year, thus receiving performance incentive awards. Their staff willingly accepts extremely difficult assignments and produce quality products. Their vision is to be customer-oriented and they have honored that vision." Ms. Debbie Sanders, Contracting Officer, USDA.

"ITX has been a great company to work with and is always responsive to our needs." Mike Sieg, Branch Chief, USDA, Fort Collins.

"Thank you ITX for installing our new ShoreTel VoIP system. Our users are simply delighted, it works and features are so much better than our old phone system." Margaret Brocklander, IT Director, City of Brighton, CO.

"Thank you ITX for providing us great IT service for 10 years." Kim Allen, CFO, The Group, Inc. Real Estate.

"Based on feedback obtained from various customers, ITX's performance is above the MAQL for timeliness, accuracy, and quality...therefore the performance indicators determined ITX to receive 100% incentive payout." James Dickey, Contracting Officer, Western Area Power Administration.

Additionally, Mai is recognized internationally. He was featured on the front cover of a Vietnamese national magazine, Doanh Nhan, December 2007 issue, as a successful businessman about whom they did a feature story.

*I believe that ITX lives up to their mission statement—it's not just a written statement. Their mission statement is a daily practice: "Our mission is to deliver **best-value IT solutions** by partnering with our clients to help them achieve their goals. We provide quality products, solutions, and services—on time, within budget." I think Bruce Hottman's statement illustrates their commitment to and relationship with their customers: "When Mai and I started ITX, we executed our business plan as expected. The one thing I never counted on was developing such great relationships with our customers. I know now that our business is about relationships, and we do everything we can to strengthen those relationships."*

Mai is a man who has developed the skills for operating a successful business from "the school of hard knocks" and the support of friends and family along his journey. What one foster family provided for him in Fort Collins, Colorado, has now turned into a remarkable company providing jobs for more than 140 families. Mai always believed what appears as dark and dreary must have light. He found the light, and now, he lights up the lives of many family members, employees, and friends, who are the core of his business.

I've always said that it's not about building walls and barriers, but it's about building on people. Mai builds on people. He values employees, constantly reminds himself of where he came from, and relates to whether he was treated with or without dignity. His philosophy is that we should always use the art of negotiation whether hiring, firing, or selling the product and services. Every year, Mai and his wife, Sue, make a trip to his homeland, Vietnam, not only to visit with family, but also to offer economic trade with other small businesses and donate computer equipment or funds to an orphanage.

Mai lives up to a great Japanese proverb: "Vision without action is only a dream. Action with no vision is a nightmare." I have great admiration for his triumph and for his being a living example of how to earn respect from his employees, customers, and community leaders.

On one hand, this book is about the ITX story, but realistically, it is Mai Tran's journey, and the journey has not ended.

SMALL/FAMILY
BUSINESS OF
THE YEAR 2007

ITX
INFORMATION TECHNOLOGY EXPERTS, Inc.

Fort Collins nominates favorites

See the best of the best
special pull-out section / Business

BEST
IN BUSINESS

THURSDAY
FEBRUARY 21, 2008

FORT COLLINS
COLORADOAN

THE FORECAST
THE FUTURE
LOOKS BRIGHT!

WWW.COLORADOAN.COM   A GANNETT NEWSPAPER

Customer satisfaction drives ITX's growth

By JASON KOSENA
JasonKosena@coloradoan.com

When Mai Tran and Bruce Hoffman started ITX 12 years ago in Fort Collins they never dreamed their success would sprout at the rate it has.

With an average growth of 31 percent a year that has increased to about 50 percent in recent years, their software and network support company has been on an uphill climb from day one.

"I think our success has been largely due to our philosophy that customer satisfaction in the most important part of what we do as well as employee satisfaction," said Tran, ITX's president and CEO. "We have hired good people along our way and we train them well in order to serve our customers well."

ITX is the Coloradoan's 2007 Best in Business winner in the small/family owned business category.

About 40 percent of ITX's business is in the commercial sector with the other 60 percent coming from government contracts including technical support for the United States Department of Agriculture, Department of Energy and Department of Defense, among others.

"I think the market we are in is beneficial to our success," said Hoffman, the company's executive vice president.

"Servicing the government in so many capacities has allowed us to leverage that in order to get more business in the commercial sector. Things have worked out well for us, but it didn't come without a lot of hard work."

Hard work is an understatement.

Before the company really got off the ground, both Tran and Hoffman, as well as many of Tran's family members, worked 70- to 80-hour weeks just trying to keep up.

Starting up in Fort Collins, a tech-heavy community has been beneficial, they admit.

"Fort Collins has been more than great for us," Tran said. "People who own small businesses here want to work with other small businesses." Added Hoffman, "I think having such a well-educated and technical community of people in Fort Collins has helped as well. There are a lot of people here who do what ... we do. That means we have a lot of

competition but it also means we have a large pool of people to hire from."

ITX also recently opened an office in Greeley last year.

The family-owned company also did

ITX Inc. owners Mai Tran, left, and Bruce Hoffman built their company from the ground up. ITX Inc. is the 2007 Small/Family Business of the Year.

$20 million in government contracts alone last year — a figure Tran and Hoffman are proud of but one they say is only part of what they do.

"Small businesses are our bread

and butter," Tran said. "They always have been and we will always focus on working with them. Really, we know how to serve them because we are one."

Appendix A

Mai Tran's Outward Bound Diary

MAi-ANH TRAN
_____
NAME

_____
COURSE

_____
PATROL

OUTWARD BOUND

TO SERVE TO STRIVE AND NOT TO YIELD

COLORADO

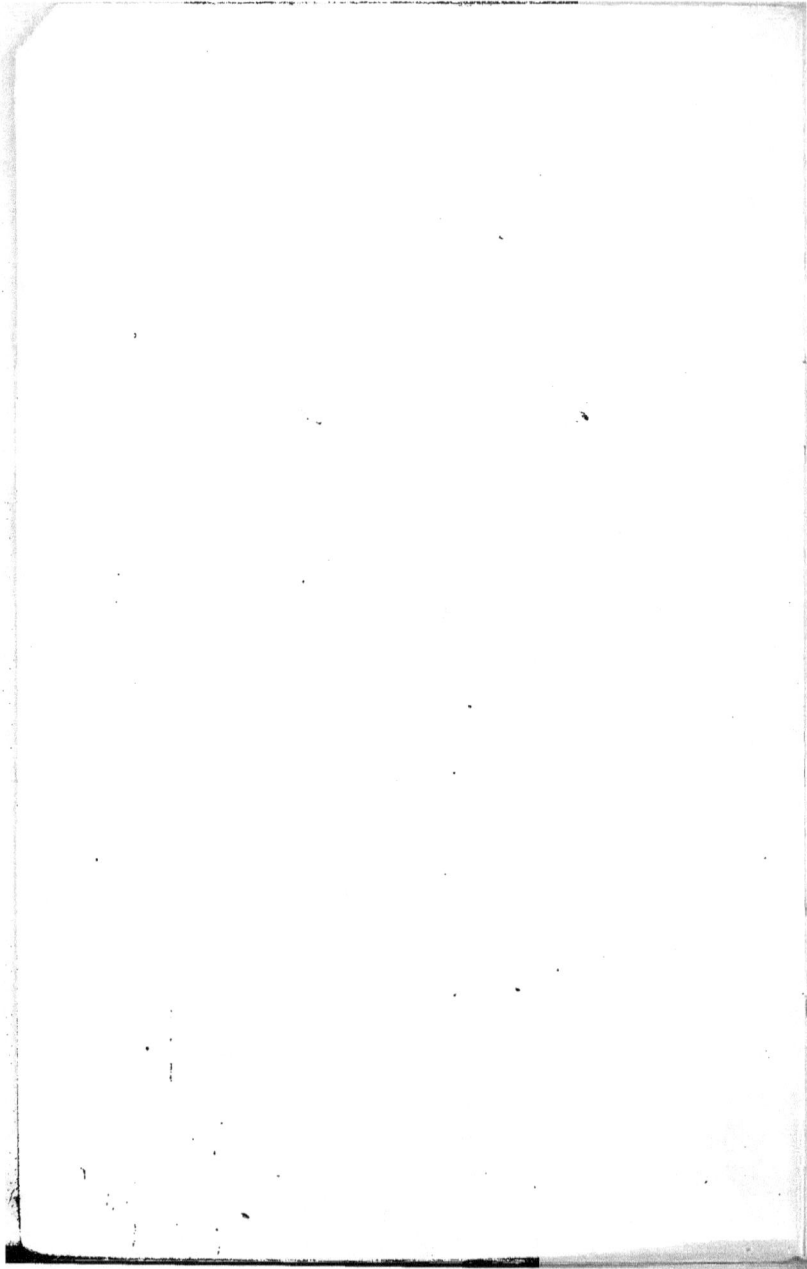

MAI

ANH

TRAN

OUT

WARD

BOUND

Dear mom

It is a Book I wrote for you my second mather, I wemt you know what I clid in 22 clays OUTWARD Bound. wRat I tRougtR aBout you. I wamt to you know me unselertant me and Pike me. I have only one think to Iall with you ; I miss you very much in 22 clays outward Bound.

June - 20. 1980

after I leff my mom, Dad and TH, I went to Durango by Bus. I met 20 more peoples and we are to gether in a group, it name is GONGO I don't know why It has this name.

we start to go on a top of a mountain, I am very tired, I can't think I walk and carry 40 pounds.. I walk about 4 Rours and stop It is 8 o'clock. we eat Dup But It is not look like a Dup, after we ate we go to sleep in a sleep in Beg

I sleep outside, we don't have a top for tonigth, But I don't care Because I am very tired and very cold. It is rainning too. I can't sleep I miss my mom my sitter I want to go Rome It is not fun, It look like wen I lived on a Boat.

The fist day of 22 days

June - 21 - 1980

In a morning I get up 8 o'clock, I think I am
Im my room, I am wrong, I am in my sleep
im Beg. I miss my famille my mom, dad very
much. I stay far from them about too miles
I can't see them now. we are eating breacfeast
with chocolat milk and some thing I can't
eat because it is very new for me.
Today we walk more but we don't walk
too far, about 3 miles. I helps one girl carry
earn her pack, she can't walk any more becau-
-se she is very tired, me too, but I want to
to help some people, I like it. we stop on
top of a man hill near the mountain name
is Camby, Ithas too much snow.
A hill where we stay, It has a mine very
old, we can't sleep inside. Tonigth I go
to sleep with 5 more peoples im my groups.
we sleep in a smalle top. I am happy be-
-cause my teacher and 3 more girls they
can speak French. it is very cold.

June - 22 - 1980

Today we get up early 6 o'clock, after we eat bracfeast we walk more near a mountain. My teacher teach me how walk on snow, if I fall dow how do I stop fall. It is fun because look like I ski on snow.

After I learn that we begin to climb on top of a mountain.

When I stay on top and I look dow, I am very surprise because I don't believe I can do that. It high 12.00 feet, after we got on top, we walk more about 5 miles, It is a hard walk too. Six o'clock we stop near a river, we want to go througth it but we can't. It is very deep, almost 7 inches. we have to stop and make a top here. Tonigth we sleep here and we will across a river tomorow. Tonigth we eat beef and chicken, I cook it, I like a meal tonigth, But the peoples in my group they don't like it.

In camp HongKong we tryed to go USA , we
Know we can go to more (and) my parents
they wanted we do that too . when I came
Denver we didn't Rave some body pick us
up, we don't Be affrait , we don't scare But
I was sad . I didn't Know Row we lives
and where do we stay .
The first time I met you , I Pike you , I Pike
your gers I Pike your Rair and I think you
can Relp us . Now It is rigth , you try to Relp
us very much . I don't Know Row to tolet say
thank you . we need famille and you gave us
famille . Some . Body think us need food , they
are
was wrong , we need some Body love and Pike
us , we didn't Rave it 4years in camp , now
you are giving for us all this . You understant
us Pook Pike my mather . I want to Pive with
you all my Pife I don't want to Peave you,
any more . I can't do that Because I Rave my
country and my famille But I think I will
stay with you when you are old : I Pove you
I Pike you very much , I Pook you same my mather
Rell this sentences I wrote It is my mind , But I
want to Know Row do you think about us.
Bye mum M

Dear mom

Tonigth I want to write for you, I know you can't read what is I am writing, but i lik to write for you. I and my sitter, we eelp my our famille almost 2 yars, we are very soff sad. Six months we lived on a skyluc we met to many people not good. They hartt me and TH to much, when we were picking, we didn't have any people help us. TH, she cryed very much, I wanted to cry too but, if I was crying I could not stop her crying. I was biger than I lived with my famille, I am stronger than I lived with my parents because I Roul TH my yonger sitter. She is very soff and she doesn't know not thing I have to help and gardian her. 2 years ago we look like a baby Birds com't fly in a big sky. Six months we lived on a ship, we wrote many letters for our cousins and our friends, I thougth they will help us but they didn't alswer. I don't want to see they any more.

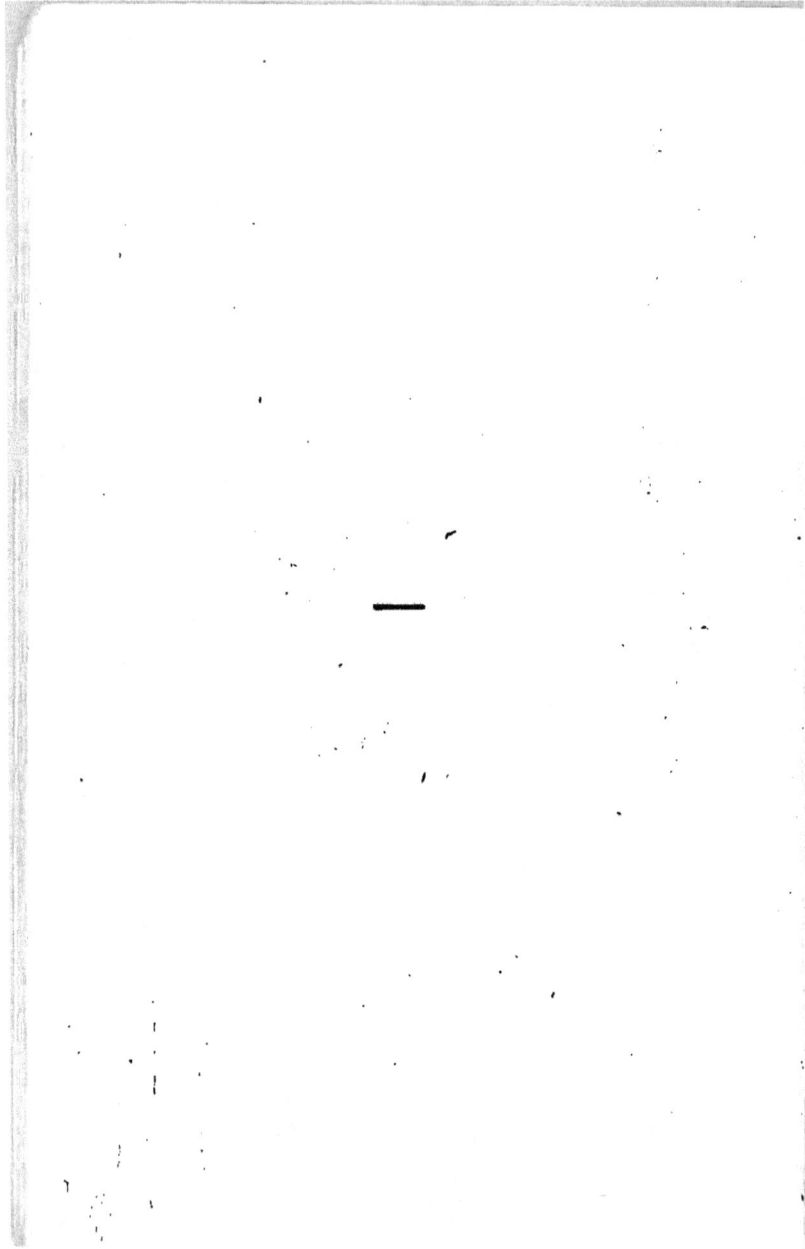

June . 23 . 1980

To day we walk about 5 miles . we walk on a trail against a creek, and we go through a creek. All my fingers get hurt, my feet too, I don't know why, but I think Because It is very cold.

To nigth we six together and talk. The peop in my group want to know why? I came USA? why I left VN. I tell with them about communiste, what did communiste did in viet NAM whe they toke over.

I like to do that, my parents and my mom I think they like and Believe me too.

I choosed to go OUTWARD BOUND Because I want to come back VN and my countri It has many forest and mountain, I have to know all that if I want to do REVOLVTI I will do that if VN has communiste and if I Breathes and live.

we stay in that place 2 nigth, we will go ontop a mountain and we rappell on a cliff rock tomorow.

good nigth.

M

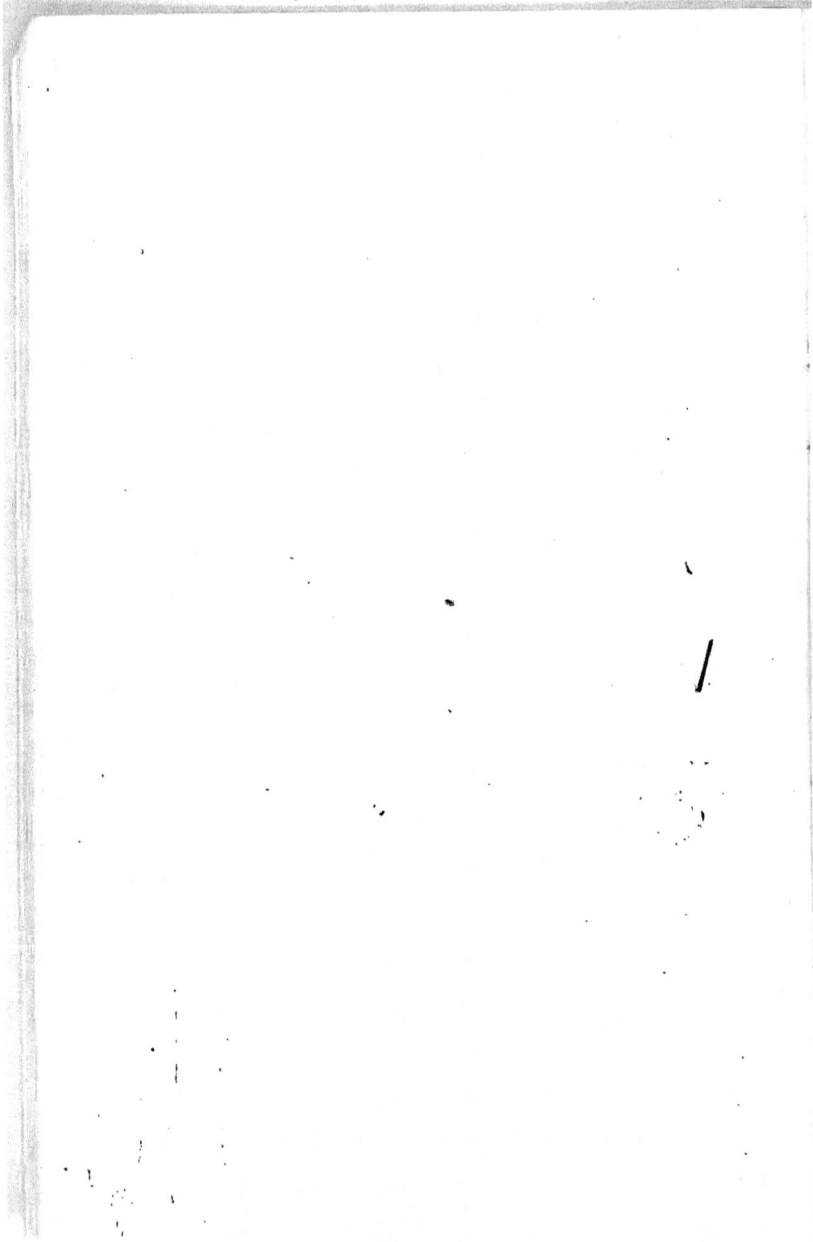

June 24, 1980 –

To day I go on top a mountain, I see a nother group OUTWARD BOUND, they are going on tof too. My teacher, he choose the place for the rappell.

when I am rappelling I can't look clow, the rock very cliff. I don't scare it I like it. One girl in my group shi is scare it and she doesn't rappell.

Affter we rappelled we come back accamp and we sleep here 1 more nigth. I get six today I want to throw up, I miss mom and my mather, if now I have them I don't have to lay clow with my seef and heny I am very sad, I want to go home, I want to see mom and TH, I love them very much, They are staying in my hand, I never foget them. I think the peoples they are not good friend for me, they don't want to talk with me, they eat, they don't call me and some thing no good more but I don't want to write clow. I don't care, I try to stay with them some days more and I will devide, I come back the house with my famille.

June 25 1980

Today is hard day we walk very far about 12 miles. I am very tired. we have to walk at nigth and we stop about 12 o'clock.

The place we are staying It is a hill and that hill has the old house. I think this house had many years ago. Tonigth is the fist day we go to sleep in a house.

My teacher he told with us, we will get food to morow 3 o'clock.

I want to write for mom now

Hi mom, how are you doing, what are you doing, tonigth I can't sleep because I miss you. I think now you are sleeping or you are watching a TV. Do you miss me, today I was very tired. I will write a letter and sent for you tomorow.

I want to talk with you, I will tell you every thing I saw It is very surprise for you, but I can't see you. I am very sad now. The peoples in my group, they are sleeping, It has a mun tonigth. I am sisting and look at a mun.

June 26 1980

Today is good day, we walk about 4 miles and we meet a car bring food for us. I want to go home today, In my group 2 girls, they are going Rome. I am very sad because I don't have friend, It is not fun with me any more, I need famille now. I am choosing stay or go Rome.

I change my mind, i will stay with mountain and forest, I want to go Rome too but I don't want the peoples in my group my teacher. They think I am scare tired. I try to stay here 2 more weeks. I will see TH and mom after 2 mor weeks. I sented letters for mom and dad, TH, I hope they get my letters very soon. They pack, It is very havy, I have to carry to much food.

I can't eat dinner tonight, I can't eat the food they make. I am going to sleep.

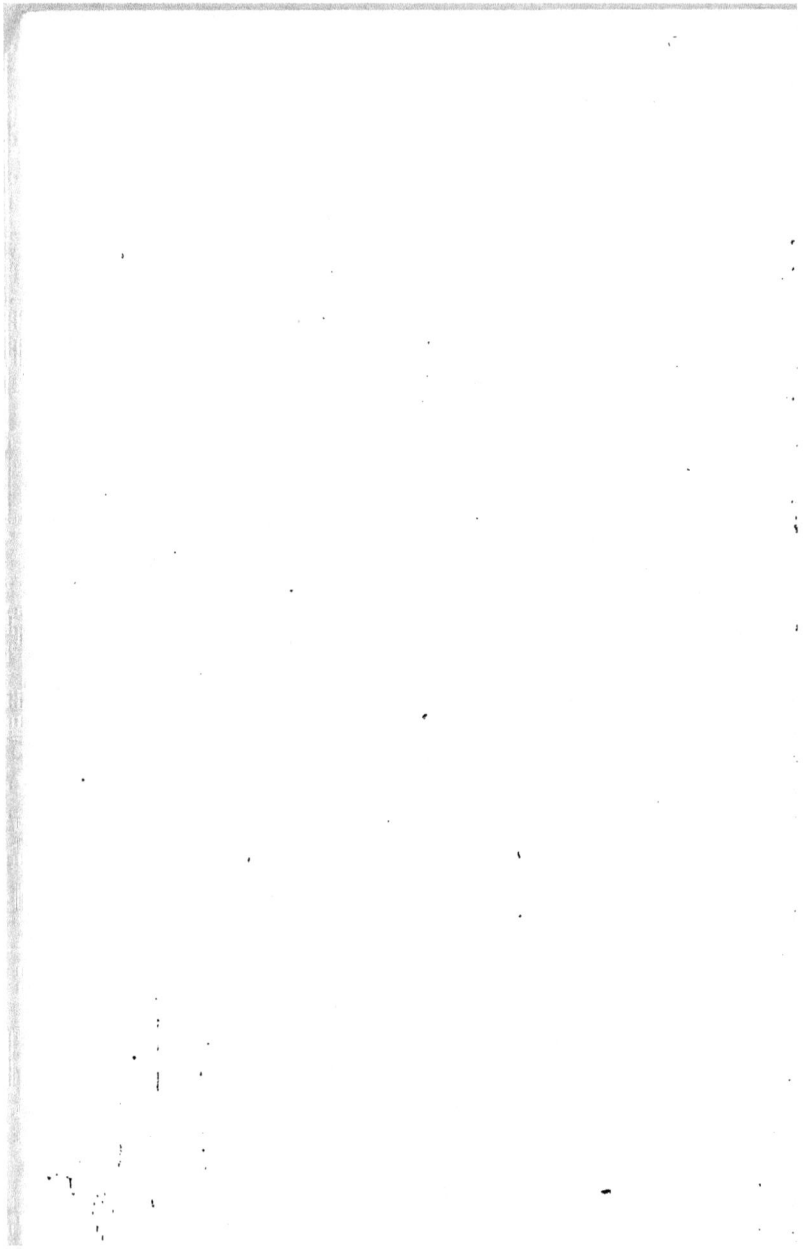

June 27 1980

we went wrong way today, we have to walk to far, we walked through the mountain and the forest. my teacher has to look for us. we went on top mountain, It has a Big lake, and the water fall.

I was very sad, I try to talk with they but I can't, I don't know why? I think because I have a Black hair, I am not america. They look me funny, I don't like, I go to sleep soon when they are together.

I want to talk with my teacher about that and I tell with him I want to go home but I...???

I buy medecine for my fingers and 3 more roles film for my camera, I toke many pic-- tures, I have only one thing to do, take a pic-- tures, I don't talk, I don't laugth any more. I want to give mom & dad my pictures when I come back. .

my god, help me, I try to finish OUTWARD Bou I am thinking about my famille in VIETNAM I hope they have a food and they are happy I think they are getting my gif.

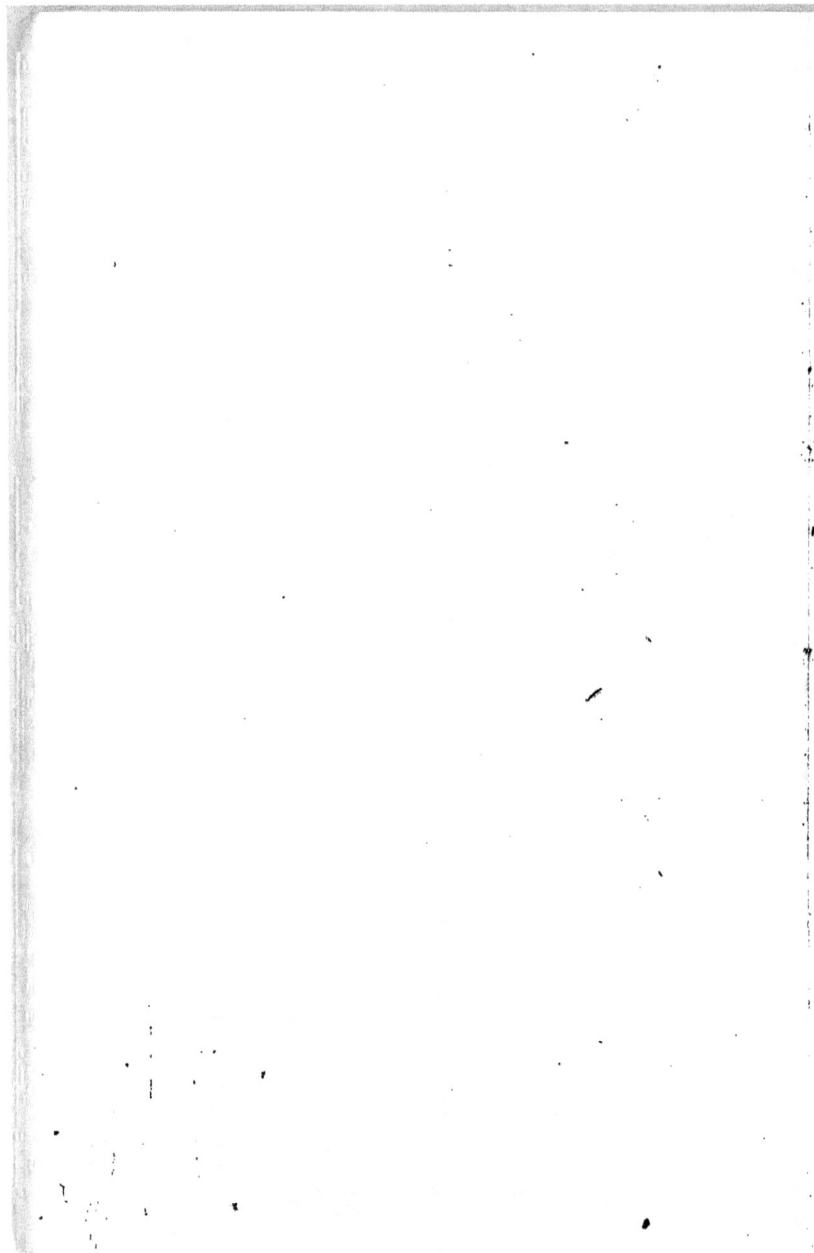

june 28 1980

I get up this morning, I am very sad, I want to go home rigth now, I don't want to stay Here any more. I didn't see fun wRen I walked, I ate. I miss my sitter and mom. If I Ban fly I will fly to them. I miss my friend. ALL the peoples I knew in FORT COLLINS, they don't laugth me wRen I was wrong, they don't look me funny. I loved FORT COLLINS very much beca It Ras my mom my sitter and all the peopl I like.

I want to cry now but I can't Because I didn't cry any more. I don't want they think Vietnammese solf. I Rave to know, I leff VN and live with a nother country, the peoples in this country many don't like me, because I am refuge I don't Rave a Rouse and famil They don't know, I am Raving a new famille with mom & Dad 5 Brothers and 1 sitter. My famille I think they me very much, I don't need the peoples in my groups any more.

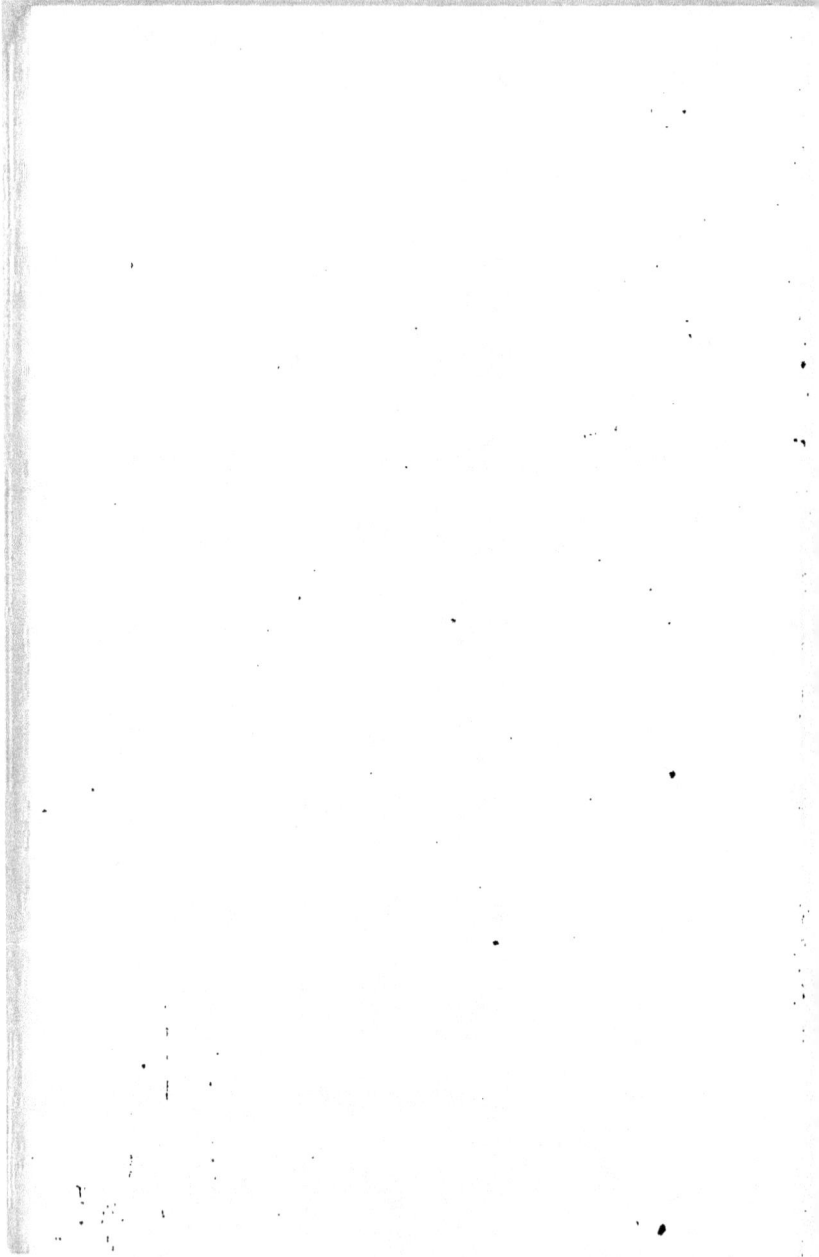

June 28 1980

we climb on top of a mountain, it is very steep, I don't scare it, but I get sick because It is very high for me (1300)

we are camping on a good place, I take many pictures. To nigth we eat sup, after I eate, I go to talk with my teacher about the peoples in my group and I talk with him I want to go home.

To day is a day 10 for out ward bound I have to try 12 more days and I com back, I am very happy if I think about that. I will see mom and my sitter very soon. Now I want to Know what are they doing, are they happy, I hope they are very happy Because they are a good famille, I was Kappy when I lived with them.

I want to hear Denny say "see that" I miss him very much, I look him like my brother. How Do I see every body in my famille now. MY GOD??? !!!

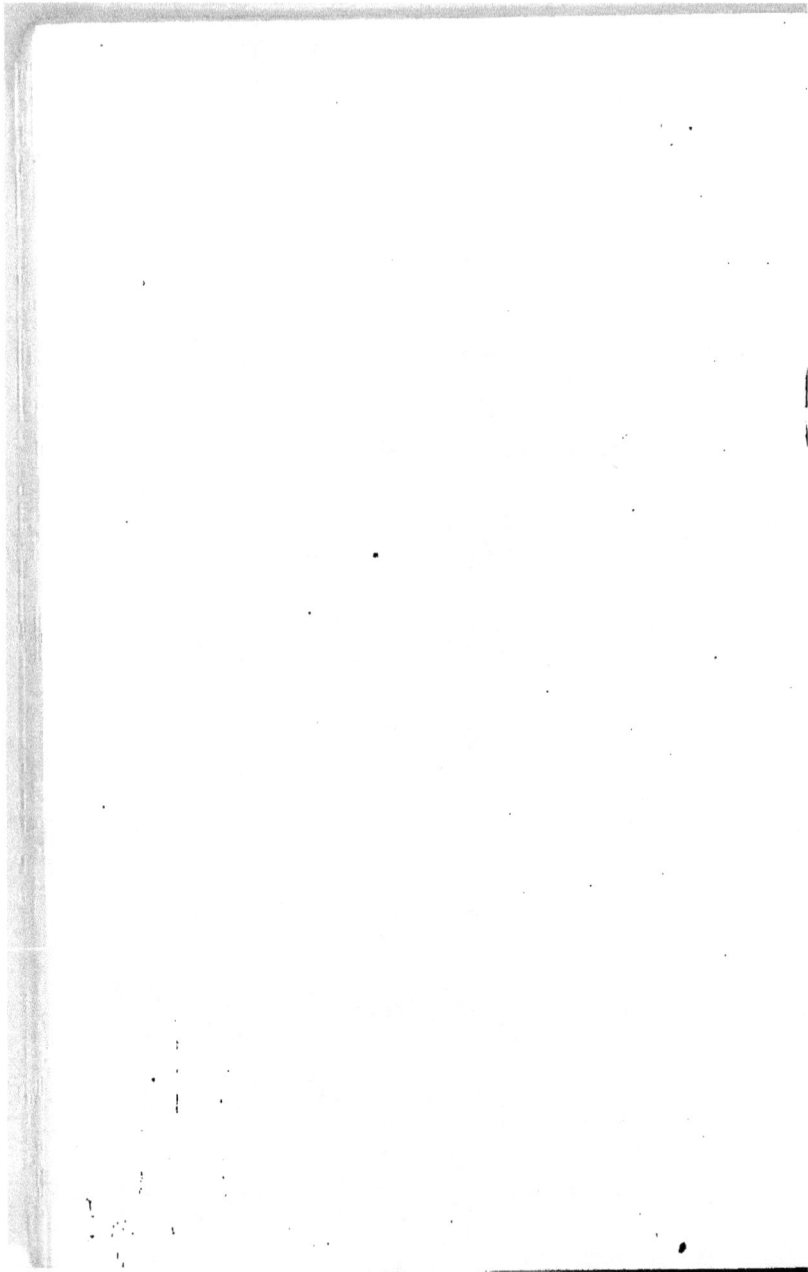

June_30_1980

Last nigth I was dreaming I saw I came back
FORT COLLINS, I talked with mom and TH
I saw they were very happy to saw me and
me too, I ate dinner with them, It was
very good food, I liked very muck. I Rad
chicken and, Beef and salad. I am Komy now
I am thinking about I ate last nigth.
To day we don't Rave to walk to far from
the camp, we come back a camp we went
to sleep last nigth. we climb on tof of a
nother agcint it nam is PEAK ONE (1378)
I like this place very much, I want to stay
here I don't want to move any more, It is
very beautyful, I think if mom, she see it
she will like it too.
I have to leave this plas tomorow afternoon,
now I am going to look for the flowers for
mom and my sitter. I like a violet flowers, I
will tak One for mom and one for TH. I think
They will be happy if they get it.

June _ 82 _1980

we have to get up early to day, we leave
a camp 6, 30. I climb ontop of a nother
mountain . It high 2889 feet . After that
we walk 3 miles in a forest, it is rainning
all my body get wate , I am very cold.
Tonigth I eat rice and chicken , they make
is not good , but I am Penny , I have to eat.
To nigth I go to sleep soon because we will
walk hard tomorow.
The peoples in my group , they are talking and
they laugth to much , I can't sleep.
I am thinking more about my sitter and mom,
if now I am stay in Rome , I think we are
talking , I like to talk with mom . Stle
unstertant me . I don't want to talk with
the people in my group , they are not nice ,
they think they are top and I am low.
If I can go Rome I will going Rome rigth now.

MRAH

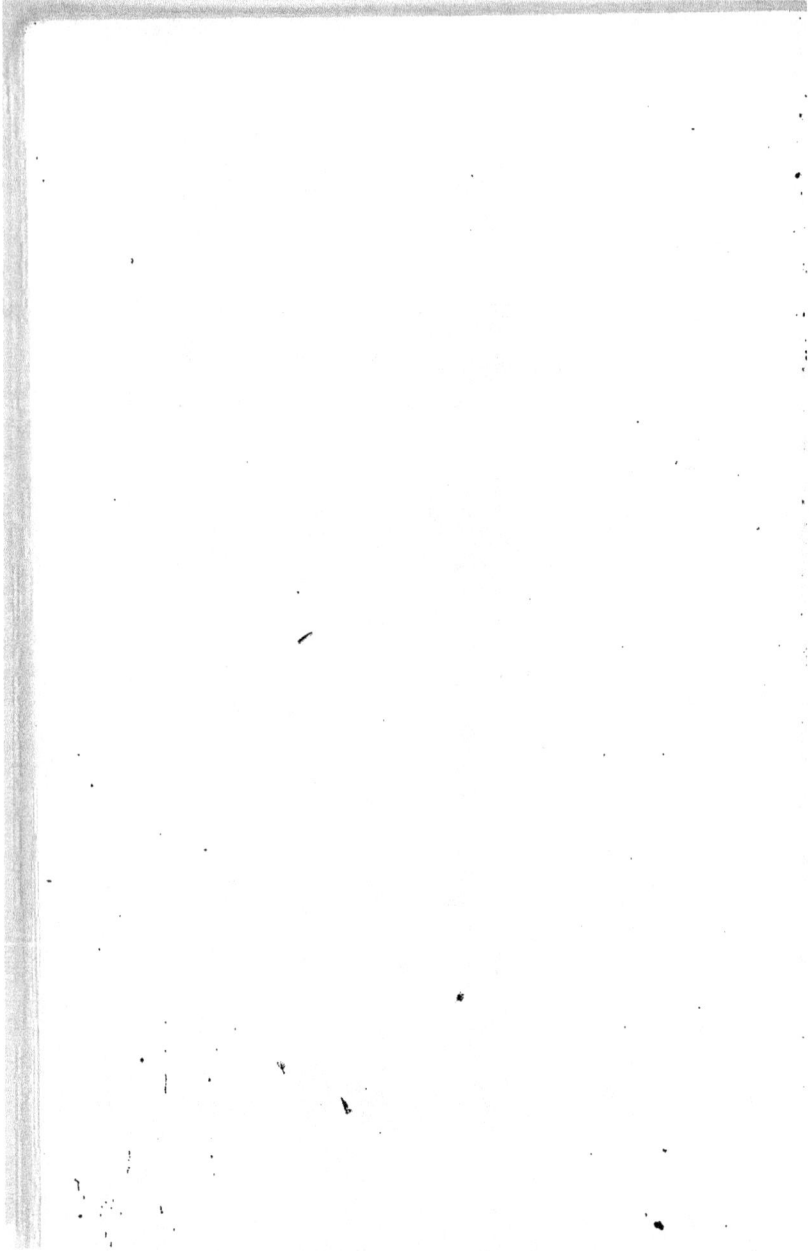

July 1 1980

Today I walk 5 miles, It is rainning too.
I am angry the girl in my group, she is name
Dabbie. She thinks I have to litten hear her, if
she want stop I have to stop, I can't do if
I want. She thinks she very smart.
I don't like her and I won't talld with her
anymore.
I have to walk 1 more day, after tomorow
is the day solo, after 3 days solo is 3 days
for test final, one day for run 10 miles and
eat final dinner, one day... I go Home
to nigtk is the last day my group go to sleep
to gether, I don't care about that because I
was not happy in my group
I like to go outward bound very much but
I don't want to stay with my self look like
I am now.
I had the violet flowers I will give her. I don't
know why? I like her very much, I don't want
to leave her any more, she is my second mal her.

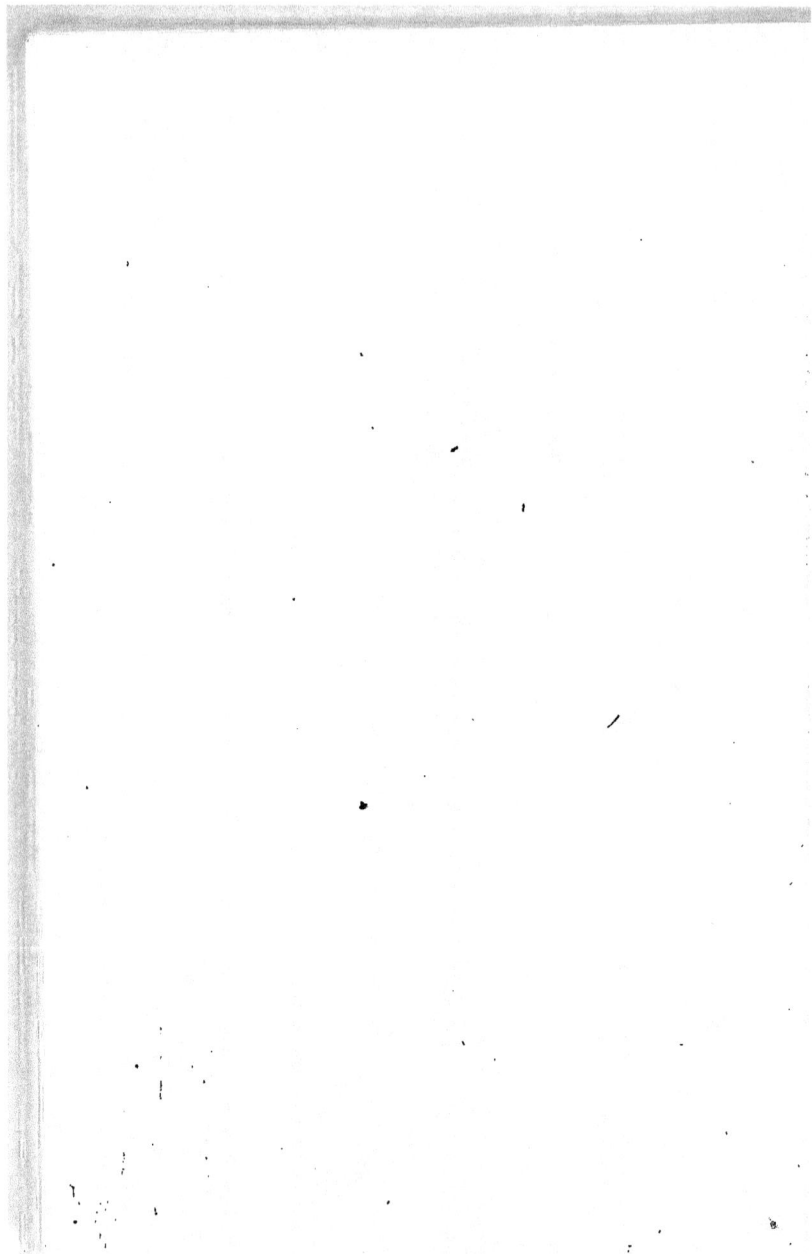

July 2 1980

Last night we sleeped in a good mines. It is a Best place we have. After noon today after we walk 6 miles we will devide and go solo 3 days.

we get a little food solo, I can eat this food for 1 meal But i have to eat for 3 days, I think I will be Henry. I don't care Henry because I was Henry 6 months on my ship.

I like to go solo, I will have a times for thinkin and take a Break.

The Lunch meal today we eat all the food we are haveny and we devide the group for solo. After 3 days solo I will have a new gray I hope the peoples in my new group, they like me and they want to make friend with me.

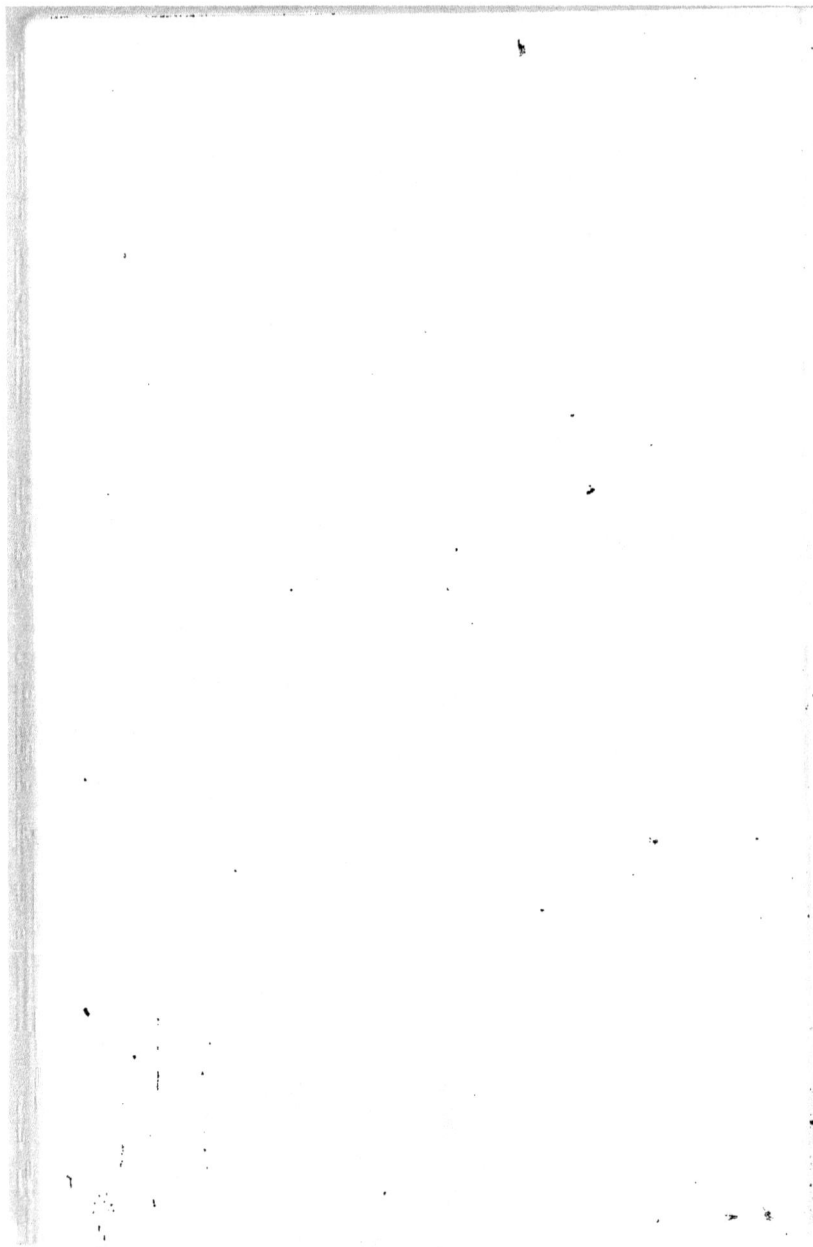

July 8 1980

we begon to go solo after noon yesterday,
I make a top for me, I lay dow in this top
all day, I am thinking many thing (my life,
my famille in VN and my new famille)
I am Renzy. I think if I go Rome I will eat
much food. I like the foods mom cooked.
It is bood like when I was living in a ship
no food, no friend and no famille But I have
my sitter I love her very much, I know she
miss me too.

July 8 1980

I get sick, I am Renzy, I couldn't go to sleep
last nigth Because I was Renzy very much.
I dreamed I saw mom cooked many foods,
but I can't eat that foods Because I got up
I am angry me, I want to go sleep more but
I can't. I Rope I dream more tonigth and I
eat very quicly and I wont get up early any more

Aug - 5 - 1980

I can't sleep cast nigth, my ear gets hurt very much, I wont to scream Because et hs hurt to much. I go to sleep about 3 o'clock in a moiming. To day is a last day for solo we will get together to nigth.

Afternoon my teacher go to get me and I have a good clinner (chicken rice, chocolat milk, Apple banana) I am not henry any mor, on Boy he can't walk Because he is Henry.

3 days don't eat I was henry too But if I think about my peoples the refuges they are going on a see, they don't know when they get a food, when they get a land, they are henry alots than me.

The Peter he told maybe tomorow after we get some more food I go to doctor for my ear. I hope I can call mom, I can hear she talk. I miss her very muck. Tonigth I have to go sleeps out a top, It does not have wom form me any more. I will Be call

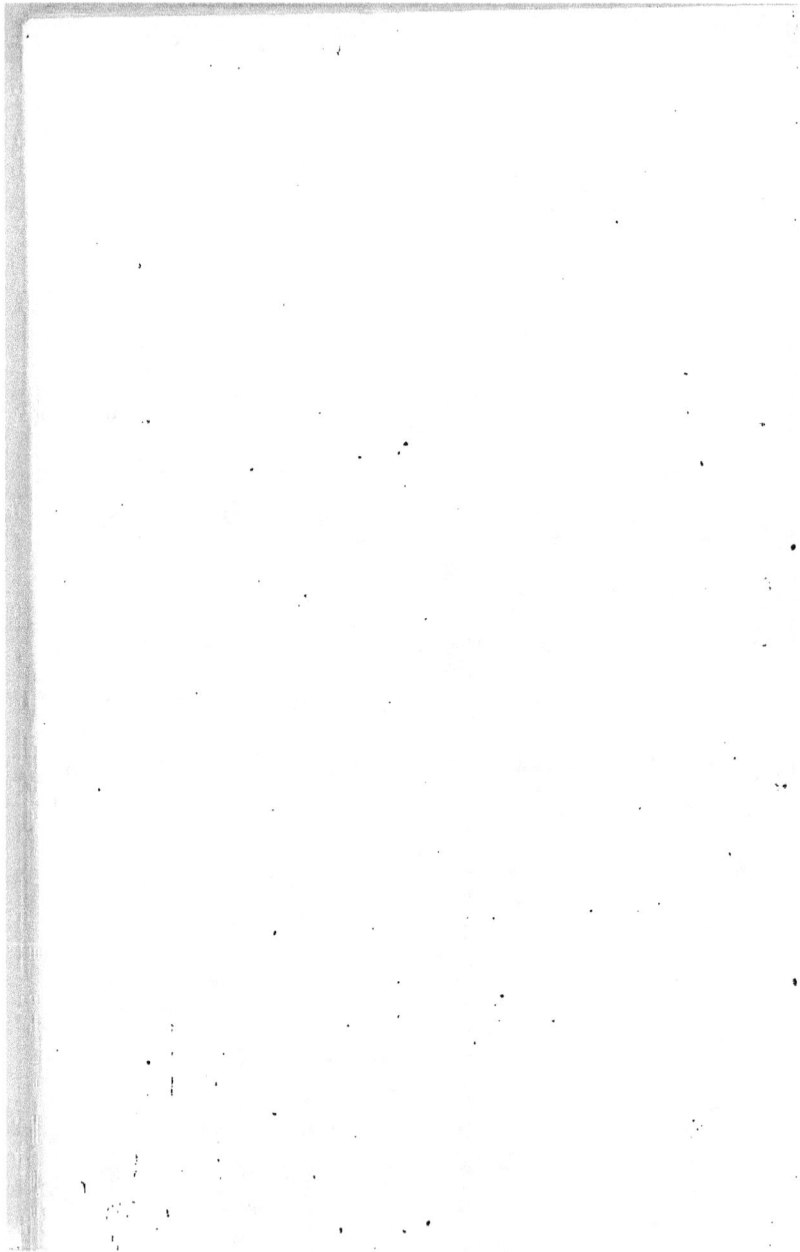

July - 6 - 1980

we Begin to walk 8 o'clock Because we have
to meet a track Brings food for us 10 o'clock.
will
Iv meet a new peoples after I get food and
I will make a new group.
My group has 6 peoples.
I go dow to SILVERTON and I go to doctor
I will meet my group tomorow morning
very well
I called mom, But I can't hear Because
my ear hurt. I will meet her 4 more days.
I can't wait to see her.

June 7 1980

To day is good day, I learn about flowers
animals and trees I like it. 51ry group they
are nice to me too. Tomorow I will walk
hard, I have to go over 3 of the mountains
but the day after tomorow is easy day
and I will see mom and TH in a morning
saturday. I love it. I have to try 3 more
day. I am happy now because I will
come back a house very soon i don't have
to wait long time any more..

I don't know how many times I reacled,
moms letters. now I can remember all about
she wrote. I love her very much.
I will read it more, this letter help
me very much, I don't feel tired any mor
if i read it.

June 8 1980

Today is hard day too, we lost today, we
go up and go clow many time but we didn
see a trail.

we begin to walk #o'clock and we stop8
o'clock evening we can't climb clow any mor
because it is very very steep. My byter have
to get me but we can't goclow, it is very
dark, I have to go sloep on a mountain
no top with 1 more girl in my group, I don'
eat dinner today and I am very cold.

June - 9 1980

I kant go to sleep last nigth because It was very cold and I didn't have a place for lay dow.

I have to rappell to go clow, It is not hard I like to rappell, It is fun. The day fter tomorow I will see mom and TH, I don't have to walk tofar more but tomorow we have to run 14 miles I think I can't but I try and we will have a big dinner for final.

July 11 1980

Today we begin to run 7,30 o'clock, we have to talk of the shore and take on it and run. we run up on a mountain and run down, 15 miles I can't think I can do that but I did with 2 hours and 34 minutes

afternoon we have final dinner, give back every things we borowed and we will go to grand JS 7 o'clock by bus tomorow.
I don't believe out ward Bound is over.
MY God today is last day of outward Boun

Appendix B

Second Indochina War Statistics

Second Indochina War (1960–75): 3,500,000
Vietnam War (1965–73): 1,700,000
http://users.erols.com/mwhite28/warstat2.htm#Vietnam

Most historians of the Second Indochina War concern themselves primarily with the American phase of the conflict, 1965–73; however, many do not specify whether their estimated death tolls cover only this phase of the war or the whole thing. An asterisk (*) indicates that the number seems to cover the entire conflict rather than just the American phase:

o **South Vietnam military**
- 181,483 (Gilbert).
- 185,000 to 225,000 (*Britannica*).
- 220,357 (Lewy, *Encyclopedia Americana*).
- 223,748 (Summers; also 3 April 1995 *AP*).
- 224,000 (Kutler, Olson).
- 250,000 (Clodfelter, Grenville*).
- 254,257 (Wallechinsky*, COWP (Correlates of War Project) [1965–75]).
- 650,000 (Small & Singer).

MEDIAN: 224,000.

- o **North Vietnamese military and Viet Cong**
  - 444,000 (*Encyclopedia Americana*).
  - 500,000 (S&S).
  - 660,000 (Olson).
  - 666,000 (Lewy, with the possibility that as many as 222,000 (one-third) of these were SVN civilians mistaken for VC).
  - 666,000 (Summers).
  - 700,000 (COWP (Correlates of War Project) [DRV 1965–75]).
  - 700,000–1,000,000 (Wallechinsky*).
  - 900,000 (*Britannica*; Grenville*).
  - 922,290 (Gilbert [NVN soldiers and civilians and VC]).
  - 1,000,000 (Clodfelter).
  - 1,100,000 (Tucker*, Official VN* [1954–75]).

  MEDIAN: starred*: 1,000,000; unstarred: 666,000.

- o **South Vietnamese civilians**
  - 50,000 (Gilbert).
  - 250,000 (Olson).
  - 287,000 (Clodfelter = 247,600 war deaths plus 38,954 assassinated by NLF).
  - 300,000 (Kutler; Summers).
  - 340,000 (Lewy's estimate, with the possibility that an additional 222,000 counted as VC (above) belong in this category).
  - 430,000 (The Senator Edward Kennedy Commission, according to Lewy, Olson).
  - 522,000 (Wallechinsky*).
  - 1,000,000 (*Britannica* [in both North and South]; Eckhardt; Grenville*).
  - 2,000,000 (Tucker*, Official VN* [N&S, 1954–75]).

  MEDIAN: starred*: about 1,500,000. unstarred: 300,000.

○ **North Vietnamese civilians: 65,000 (Kutler, Lewy, Olson, Summers, Wallechinsky) by American bombing. Sources:**
  http://users.erols.com/mwhite28/warstat2.htm#Sources

- *Britannica*: not specified, but the implication is that the statistics cover the entire war.
- Clodfelter, Michael: *Vietnam in Military Statistics* (1995).
- COWP (Correlates of War Project): Covers 1965–75 *http://www.correlatesofwar.org/cow2%20data/WarData/InterState/Inter-State%20War%20Participants%20(V%203-0).htm*.
- Eckhardt: covers 1965–75 (unless otherwise noted).
- *Encyclopedia Americana* (2003): "Vietnam War."
- Grenville: does not specify which years are covered, but by context, it seems to be 1960–75.
- Hanson, Victor Davis: "Tet, January 31–April 6, 1968," Carnage and culture (2001).
- Kutler, Stanley: *Encyclopedia of the Vietnam War* (1996).
- Lewy, Guenter: *America in Vietnam* (1978): Lewy's estimates cover 1965–74.
- Official VN: On the 20th anniversary of the war's end, Hanoi announced its official tally of losses for twenty-one years of war: 1954–75. (Nov. 5, 2004) [*Associated Press*, April 3, 1995; *Xinhua News Agency*, April 3, 1995; *Financial Times* (London, England), April 5, 1995; *Herald Sun*, April 5, 1995; *Washington Post*, April 30, 1995; *Plain Dealer* (Cleveland, Ohio), January 1, 1996; *United Press International*, February 25, 1997.
- Olson, James: *Dictionary of the Vietnam War* (1988): Covers 1965–74.
- Summers, Harry: *Vietnam War Almanac* (1985).
- Tucker, Spencer: *Encyclopedia of the Vietnam War* (1998).
- Wallechinsky: Death Tolls apparently cover 1957–75.
- Young, Marilyn: *The Vietnam Wars: 1945–1990* (1991).

Brief Biography of the Author

Ray Martinez is dedicated to the Fort Collins, Colorado, community in which he grew up and has more than thirty years' experience in public service. He began his career in the Fort Collins Police Department in 1974 and retired in 1996. Mr. Martinez was the lead investigator in an international terrorist investigation that became the subject of two published books: *Death Merchant* by Joseph Goulden and *Manhunt* by Peter Maas. He also authored and published four books of his own. Martinez was elected mayor of Fort Collins for three consecutive terms: 1999, 2001, and 2003. He left office in April 2005 to honor term limitations. Ray hosts a weekly radio talk show on KFKA radio in Greeley, Colorado, and he still sits on several national, state, and local boards. He currently is the Director of Business Development for ITX in Fort Collins, Colorado (www.itxfc.com).

"Having a dream is the embryo to creating a vision, which is the cause of creation. Creation through a person is designed by our Creator—it's God's greatest gift to each one of us—an idea. An idea conceived is hope that becomes reality." —Ray Martinez

Other books written by Ray Martinez

A Matter of Survival, Your Fight against Burglars. ISBN 9780964465206

Saturday's Opinion. A collection of short stories covering national, state, and local issues. ISBN 9780964465220

Baby Boy-R. A memoir about Ray Martinez' search for his biological mother. ISBN 9780595447466

Growing Daily: A Forty-Day Experience. ISBN 9781414115436

Just Another Opinion **ISBN: 978-0-9644652-8-2**

Books Including Ray Martinez

The Death Merchant by Joseph C. Goulden. ISBN 0-671-49341-8

Manhunt: The Incredible Pursuit of CIA Agent Turned Terrorist by Peter Maas. ISBN 0-394-55293-8

101 Memorable Men of Northern Colorado by Arlene Ahlbrandt. ISBN 0-9663932-8-7

Modern Visions Along the Poudre Valley by Phil Walker. ISBN 1-887982-13-2

Hit from Behind...Out of Perfect Timing Came Perfect Chaos... by Jim Heckel. ISBN 978-1-60791-034-3

50 Interviews—Dream It, Live It, Love It by Don McGrath. ISBN 978-0-98229-071-2

You can learn more about Ray Martinez at www.raymartinez.com.

www.ingramcontent.com/pod-product-compliance
Lightning Source LLC
LaVergne TN
LVHW051637080426
835511LV00016B/2372